Resilience and the Management of Nonprofit Organizations

T0327594

In memory of Jeff Brudney, Russ Cargo, Sharon Oster, Fred Lane and Lester Salamon, lost to us in 2021 and 2022 but forever remembered for their friendship and unique and pioneering contributions to the field of nonprofit studies

Resilience and the Management of Nonprofit Organizations
A New Paradigm

Dennis R. Young

Emeritus Professor, Jack, Joseph and Morton Mandel School of Applied Social Sciences, Case Western Reserve University and Emeritus Professor, Andrew Young School of Policy Studies, Georgia State University, USA

Elizabeth A.M. Searing

Assistant Professor of Public and Nonprofit Management, School of Economic, Political and Policy Sciences, The University of Texas at Dallas, USA

 Edward Elgar
PUBLISHING

Cheltenham, UK • Northampton, MA, USA

Cartoons by Linda Serra
Foreword by Milton J. Little Jr.

Published by
Edward Elgar Publishing Limited
The Lypiatts
15 Lansdown Road
Cheltenham
Glos GL50 2JA
UK

Edward Elgar Publishing, Inc.
William Pratt House
9 Dewey Court
Northampton
Massachusetts 01060
USA

Paperback edition 2023

A catalogue record for this book
is available from the British Library

Library of Congress Control Number: 2022939119

This book is available electronically in the **Elgar**online
Business subject collection
http://dx.doi.org/10.4337/9781800889736

ISBN 978 1 80088 972 9 (cased)
ISBN 978 1 80088 973 6 (eBook)
ISBN 978 1 0353 2372 2 (paperback)

Printed and bound by CPI Group (UK) Ltd, Croydon, CR0 4YY

Contents

Figures and cartoons

FIGURES

CARTOONS

Tables

Boxes

Foreword

March 13, 2020 was unlike any Friday on record for me. President Donald J. Trump had just declared a national emergency concerning the Novel Coronavirus outbreak in the United States. My senior team and I were finalizing plans for United Way of Greater Atlanta's workforce to begin working remotely starting Monday, March 16. We assumed, like many Americans, that we would cocoon at home for a few weeks, perhaps a month, but certainly no longer than that. Little did any of us know how far off our predictions of when we would return were.

That morning I spoke to a United Way donor and volunteer. He is a real estate developer and owner of several local restaurants. He told me how bad things looked from his perch. What shocked me most was his prediction that by the end of the upcoming week he would have probably laid off more than 90 percent of his hourly workers. Where would they go and how would they support themselves and their families?

My mind raced as I imagined his prediction playing out across metropolitan Atlanta's service economy and among the vast numbers of other workers who could not simply work from home. Those we would soon be calling *essential workers*.

There would be other pandemic casualties. When the public schools closed, how would the children who depend on the school feeding programs for what might be their most nutritional meal(s) of the day eat? In addition, how many children lacked access to laptop computers and the high-speed internet that would be essential for their virtual learning? What about the essential workers with children? Who would care for the children so these workers could stock grocery shelves, pick up trash, work construction, and keep the hospitals and other healthcare facilities functioning? This one conversation ignited my imagination regarding the potentially devasting toll this emerging crisis could have if it lasted longer than our most optimistic guesses.

Within a matter of minutes, my counterpart at the Community Foundation of Greater Atlanta, Alicia Philipp, and I were on the telephone hastily sketching out plans for a joint Covid Response and Recovery Fund. The Fund, as we envisioned it, would raise money from foundations, businesses, individuals and public agencies. Money raised would be invested in frontline nonprofits who would be called up to help families and individuals navigate personal, financial, educational, health and other needs that would emerge from an Atlanta economy that for all intents and purposes shut down. Of special note, we would make the grants unrestricted, providing the agencies with absolute discretion to invest in ways that strengthened the resilience of the people they served and the agencies they led. In hindsight, this proved to be among the wisest decisions of all.

We agreed without hesitation that rather than our respective agencies launching their own funds, we would combine forces. We could in turn leverage our individual fundraising capabilities and prominence as anchor regional charitable organizations into a single, efficient effort. Why force donors to choose between two separate funds with common goals when together we could mobilize the caring power of the entire region to ameliorate the impacts we anticipated the pandemic would have on metropolitan Atlanta?

At the same time, I wondered how many of the essential frontline nonprofit organizations had the requisite resilience to make every pivot necessary to keep their doors open and the services available to those in need.

My professional life spans more than 30 years in nonprofit, for-profit, corporate philanthropic and government settings. My professional experiences have allowed me to examine or advise nonprofit organizations in more than 40 states in the United States as well as in Europe, South Africa, Israel, Australia and China. In addition, I have seen what real estate busts, dot.com implosions, September 11, natural disasters and the 2008 Recession have done to charitable donations and nonprofit organizations. I have tried to help some highly regarded nonprofits cope with inadequate staffing and technology infrastructure, little to no cash reserves, little or no attention to risk management planning, and the failures of boards to provide proper stewardship.

My friend Dennis Young and his colleague Elizabeth Searing have made an important contribution to the literature on nonprofit resilience. This book examines the issues, explanations and excuses behind the inadequate resilience we see among many nonprofit organizations. They also provide instructive looks into organizations that get it right. Finally, and importantly, they shed needed light on how the nonprofit capital market aids and hinders nonprofit resilience.

I have known Dennis for almost fifteen years. I had the pleasure of serving under his leadership when I was a member of the Nonprofit Advisory Board for the Andrew Young School of Policy Studies at Georgia State University. Dennis is a first-rate student, teacher and researcher of nonprofit management and has brought his vast experience, keen insights and analysis to bear.

Furthermore, as an applied researcher he has grounded his academic investigation in the practical experience of the real-world practitioners of nonprofit management he knows and respects.

I consider this book a must-read for nonprofit managers, for-profit professionals aspiring to transition into nonprofit careers, students of nonprofit management, nonprofit board members and aspirants, institutional as well as individual donors, and scholars.

I confess to being an unabashed champion of the nonprofit sector. Many of the nation's most important social movements were born or steered by nonprofits. Each year, tens of millions of people serve on their boards and donate time and treasure to their causes. Tens of millions of people are served by religious institutions, hospitals and nursing homes, universities, childcare centers, advocacy organizations, arts and cultural centers, and others.

The U.S. nonprofit sector employs millions of people a year. The economic value of its real property and its contribution to the nation's gross domestic product are in the hundreds of billion dollars annually. Nonprofits are a source of pride to communities and the people they serve and those who serve them.

That said, we cannot ignore examples of mismanagement or lack of planning by professional staff, and low expectations for how nonprofits should operate. And even among those who believe that nonprofits should behave more like for-profit businesses, we must overcome the reluctance many board members and donors have to giving nonprofits more of the tools that for-profit businesses have – adequate infrastructure, cash reserves, advertising budgets, and competitive salaries and benefit packages required to attract the best talent possible.

This long-overdue book provides a fulsome assessment of the factors that contribute to or confound nonprofit resilience. It is a vital resource for greater insight into the subject, and through its many examples provides both an honest assessment of failure and a hopeful path for building truly resilient nonprofit organizations.

Milton J. Little Jr.
President and CEO
United Way of Greater Atlanta

Preface

Nonprofit management as a distinctive field of management practice and study began to take shape in the late 1980s (O'Neill and Young, 1988). Since then tremendous progress has been made in building a body of knowledge for this field. The first-class research journal *Nonprofit Management & Leadership* is now in its 32nd year, the comprehensive *Jossey-Bass Handbook of Nonprofit Leadership and Management* (Renz et al., 2016) is now in its fourth edition, and the *Journal of Nonprofit Education and Leadership* has celebrated its tenth year of publication. Still, the field continues to struggle to find its own distinctive voice and point of view. Nonprofit management curricula have drawn on the diverse intellectual traditions of the host institutions in which they have developed, including schools of public administration and policy, business management and social work; on diverse disciplines including political science, sociology, law and economics; and on field-specific perspectives including health care, arts and culture, and higher education administration. Leaders of the field of nonprofit management education have put their various individual stamps on it, and to a degree they have coalesced (through the work of the Nonprofit Academic Centers Council) around a set of standards that articulate a wide-ranging set of skills and contextual knowledge which they believe nonprofit managers and leaders should master (Nonprofit Academic Centers Council, 2016).

This evolution has been influential in bringing competence and recognition to the nonprofit management profession, as witnessed by the many hundreds of universities that now have degree and certificate programs in nonprofit management and leadership or in related fields such as social enterprise, social entrepreneurship or social innovation. Thousands of nonprofit leaders and managers now have university credentials in this field. Still, questions persist about the value of such credentials in addressing the real-world challenges facing contemporary nonprofit organizations. In fact, university programs in nonprofit management education remain largely a variety of mixes and adaptations of teaching and subject matter from public administration and business management curricula, overlaid with theory and data, developed over the last four decades, descriptive of why nonprofit organizations exist in a market economy and in democratic societies. Little really holds these curricula together except the use of nonprofit examples and applications to illustrate and apply methods and ideas adopted from business and public administration, along with articulation of a value system that distinguishes the private pursuit of social mission from profitmaking business or public sector governance.

The result has been an ad hoc approach to nonprofit decision making that leaves uncertain the principles managers should follow to administer their finances, develop their resources, evaluate their performance, manage their paid and volunteer staff, cultivate relationships with stakeholder groups, or innovate and advocate for social change. Mainly, nonprofit managers have been taught to adopt broad, vague and sometimes errant notions of efficiency and mission impact to guide the work of their organizations. These often exist without a common understanding of what it takes to make their organizations successful.

Sometimes, however, the world has a way of teaching us lessons that our introspection and best efforts to build on existing knowledge may fail to do. I believe this to be the case of the recurrent economic, social and organizational crises that have rocked nonprofits in the 21st century and earlier. From the terrorist attacks on September 11, 2001 through the 2020–2021 coronavirus pandemic and its continuing economic and social repercussions, nonprofits have largely had to improvise their responses in order to survive and carry on their important work, with relatively little formal or solid guidance. Nonetheless, frontline managers and leaders have often set inspiring examples that suggest a new way of conceptualizing nonprofit management. In a word, they have begun to figure out how to manage for *resilience*, not short-term or narrowly defined efficiency as some of their funders, regulators or textbooks would have them do. Resilience would ensure that their organizations have the capacity to navigate through crises so that they continue to serve their missions effectively and robustly prepare for future challenges.

I think it is especially important for nonprofit managers and leaders to find a touchstone and guiding principles of their own, not simply a hybrid of those from business or government. Businesses are clearly driven by profitmaking and market share, and government by the political process and hopefully some overriding conception of public welfare. In those sectors resilience is not the primary issue. While some businesses try to grow large enough to ensure their permanence, most do not ultimately succeed over the long run. Indeed, we celebrate competition and "creative destruction" in business as a source of success for the market economy. Neither is resilience the touchstone for government, at least in developed countries. Government has access to taxation which ensures its permanence and longevity. Nonprofits are different. With a mix of resources from various market, voluntary and government sources, they pursue social missions by building enduring institutions to ensure the servicing of fundamental human needs including social welfare, the arts, education, health care, environmental safety, social justice, poverty relief and others. While we as a society encourage social entrepreneurship to establish new organizations where needed and to renew existing ones (see Chapter 9), we do not wish these institutions to fail. Rather we want to them to prosper so that the availability of their services is maintained through thick and thin, through crises and good times, whenever they are needed. Resilience is about more than just survival – it is also about nonprofit organizations maintaining and improving the programs and services that we are all likely to need, or have available to those we care about, at one time or another in our lives.

This book is a first effort to reframe the field of nonprofit management around the concept of resilience. It takes as given that nonprofits can and should find multiple channels through which to build margins of organizational capacity on which they can draw in a crisis and which they can put to good use in ordinary times to innovate, refresh and improve their operations and methods. Here, we call this concept "organizational slack," a notion well grounded in organizational and economic theory. Though a common misperception suggests that slack is wasteful, we argue that this is not the case. *Slack not sloth* drives our analysis, and our prescription for how to best manage nonprofit organizations for their health, effectiveness and most importantly for resilience. Our hope is that nonprofit managers, trustees and other nonprofit leaders will adopt the ideas articulated here, that funders and regulators will take them to heart, and that faculty will use them as a starting point to renovate, if not revolutionize, their curricula for educating nonprofit managers and leaders for the rest of the century ahead.

I have been personally blessed to have as my partner in this book Elizabeth Searing, my former doctoral student, and a leader in the younger generation of nonprofit management educators and scholars, who will help carry the message forward that we should be managing our nonprofit organizations for resilience so that they can effectively continue their critical work on behalf of society.

Dennis R. Young
January 2022

REFERENCES

Nonprofit Academic Centers Council (2016). *Curricular Guidelines: Graduate & Undergraduate Study in Nonprofit Leadership, the Nonprofit Sector and Philanthropy*. Cleveland, OH: Nonprofit Academic Centers Council.

O'Neill, Michael, and Dennis R. Young (1988). *Educating Managers of Nonprofit Organizations*. New York, NY: Praeger Publishers.

Renz, David O., and Associates (2016). *The Jossey-Bass Handbook of Nonprofit Leadership and Management*, 4th Edition. Hoboken, NJ: John Wiley & Sons.

Acknowledgments

We are grateful to numerous colleagues who supported our efforts to write this book, especially Thad Calabrese, Rob Fischer, Teresa Harrison, Fredrick Lane, Reynold Levy, Brian Schreiber, Richard Steinberg and Mark Young, who provided comments and suggestions on various chapter drafts.

We also want to express our appreciation to those who helped us identify and develop the organizational vignettes that we have sprinkled throughout the book, including Rikki Abzug, Rosemary Burless, Meg Cutter, Terry Davis, Will Evans, Art Falco, Lee Foster, Karen Gardner, Patty Gaul, Elizabeth Hancy, Lauren Koontz, Jack Krauskopf, Fredrick Lane, Lisa Maida, John McMicken, Amanda Minix, Katy O'Connell, John O'Kane, Lisa Purdy, Noha Ryder, Brian Schreiber and Mark Young.

We have written this book simultaneously with our participation as instructors in the National Center on Nonprofit Enterprise (NCNE) Nonprofit Resilience Management online certification program. We have benefitted from the wisdom of our fellow instructors, including Bill Waugh, Alessandra Jerolleman, Roland Kushner, Teresa Harrison, Kristina Jaskyte-Bahr, Rosemarie Emanuele, Mel Gray, Rikki Abzug and Rob Fischer. We are also indebted to Stuart Mendel, Executive Director of NCNE, for his role in overseeing the program, and to Richard Pogue for his encouragement and generous support of this initiative.

We are also grateful to Alan Sturmer and his colleagues at Edward Elgar Publishing for their encouragement and support of this work.

Finally, we would be remiss if we failed to acknowledge the patience and encouragement of our spouses, Linda Serra and Donald Searing, as we wrote this book and attempted to maintain a reasonable work–life balance.

Dennis R. Young
Elizabeth A.M. Searing

Cartoon 1   Catastrophes are so rare, we just don't worry about them!

1. Introduction to *Resilience and the Management of Nonprofit Organizations*

Nonprofit organizations are critical to the wellbeing of society, in the United States and many countries worldwide. They are not just charities in a narrow sense of agencies for helping the poor and afflicted. They educate us, keep us healthy, serve those in need, protect our environment, fight for social justice, address our spiritual and aesthetic desires, offer opportunities to give and volunteer for those of us who want to help with a myriad of social needs and causes, and work with government to improve public policy. Although there are some bad apples in the nonprofit sector, few would argue against the proposition that nonprofit organizations are deserving of our proper stewardship and support. Yet, as a society, through our behavior and our regulatory practices, and our governing and management norms, we do not treat nonprofits very well. We expect them to be paragons of virtue while often failing to provide them with the resources they need to do their jobs effectively.

The recent COVID-19 pandemic has laid bare the fact that many of our nonprofits are fragile and at risk of failing. Independent Sector (2021) reported that 40% of surveyed nonprofits experienced a loss in total revenue in 2020 and the revenues of organizations incurring those losses declined by 31% on average. Almost two-thirds of the surveyed nonprofits had to pause or suspend services during 2020. Nonprofit arts organizations were particularly hard hit. As reported by the Urban Institute (Faulk et al., 2021), the total revenue of 54% of arts organizations declined in 2020 compared to 36% for other nonprofits. The Center for Effective Philanthropy (2021) reported even higher figures from its survey: some 77% of nonprofit arts organizations suffered losses in total revenue from 2019 to 2020 compared to 51% for nonprofits overall. Most nonprofits managed to survive the crisis by radically reducing expenses (and staff), applying for government Paycheck Protection Program (PPP) loans and borrowing, among other options. Fewer than 40% were able to draw on reserve funds (Faulk et al., 2021). Some are emerging stronger from the crisis, displaying an admirable pluck and determination worthy of the finest entrepreneurial effort in any sector. But few if any nonprofits want to return to the state of vulnerability and existential risk that the pandemic exposed.

Nonprofits certainly try to stay financially healthy so that they can continue to provide services, despite having to cope with very difficult circumstances. What has become clear is that many nonprofits have been working in handcuffs, some self-applied and some externally imposed. The self-applied constraints derive from the widely accepted notion that nonprofits must continually prove themselves worthy of the charitable, volunteer, governmental and consumer support that they receive. The external constraints derive from societal expectations that if not for certain practices and policies, nonprofits would be wasteful, inefficient or dishonest – like many of our institutions in business and government. For years, Americans have been losing confidence in their institutions, and nonprofits have not been given a free pass. Hopefully, nonprofits' generally exemplary performance in the pandemic, despite the severe challenges they have faced, will contribute to an upswing in their public approval, as seems to have happened with institutions in the medical system (Brenan, 2021).

We argue in this book that a new paradigm of nonprofit management is needed to ensure that the viability and effectiveness of the nonprofit sector is maintained into the future. This is especially important because crises like the COVID-19 pandemic or the 2008–2009 economic recession, or the increasingly severe climate-related disasters of recent years, or other catastrophic events, can no longer be considered unusual or unlikely to recur in some old or new guise. While such events vary widely in their individual likelihoods and potential impacts, as we will examine in Chapter 2, together they pose significant risks to nonprofits and to society more broadly. Nor is the list of threats limited to just a few possibilities. Indeed, a recent report by the U.S. National Intelligence Council (2021) points to several underlying trends that are likely to precipitate multiple crisis situations of various kinds in the immediate future:

- Climate: "In the environment, the physical effects of climate change are likely to intensify during the next two decades … More extreme storms, droughts, and floods, melting glaciers and ice caps; and rising sea levels will accompany rising temperatures" (pp.6–7);
- Economics: "During the next two decades, several global economic trends, including rising national debt, a more complex and fragmented trading environment, a shift in trade, and new employment disruptions, are likely to shape conditions" (p.7);
- Technology: "During the next two decades, the pace and reach of technological developments are likely to increase even faster … creating new tensions and disruptions" (p.7);
- Politics: "Within societies, there is increasing fragmentation and contestation over economic, cultural, and political issues" (p.7);

- Information: "The combination of newly prominent and diverse identity allegiances and a more siloed information environment is exposing and aggravating fault lines ... undermining civic nationalism, and increasing volatility" (p.8);
- Governance: "Populations are increasingly empowered and demanding more, governments are coming under greater pressure from new challenges and more limited resources. This widening gap portends more political volatility, erosion of democracy, and expanding roles for alternative providers of governance" (p.8).

As a result of the dynamic and uncertain context in which we now live, change and uncertainty now define the frame in which nonprofit managers must operate going forward. This leads us to define a new basis for nonprofit management decision making, based on the concept of "organizational resilience." This framework does not reject the importance of probity or efficient operation, but it does give primacy to the importance of long-term viability and the capacity to anticipate, survive and even capitalize on crises and change. As such, resilience must become a fundamental organizing concept around which nonprofit management decisions and strategy are framed.

To see why this is so, we need to consider two broad factors: how nonprofits have been threatened in the recent severe crises they have faced, and how they have been hindered by current ideas about nonprofit management and the way nonprofits are externally regulated and held to account. There is also some good news here. Many nonprofits have found innovative ways to work around these challenges and limitations. We can learn from recent crisis-related experiences of nonprofits and systematize that knowledge so that all nonprofits can manage themselves with more resilience in the future. This new knowledge, forged in the crucible of crises, applies generally to the management of nonprofit organizations through time. In particular, resilience-based practices constitute a new foundation for nonprofit organizations not only to prepare and navigate through difficult times, but to thrive in good times as well.

The threats and challenges faced by nonprofits in recent crises continue to be documented. For example, various surveys and studies, if updated periodically, will be helpful in understanding the full extent of the losses and recovery from the COVID-19 pandemic. Midway through 2020, a survey by the Ohio State University and Philanthropy Ohio found that 10% of sampled nonprofits in Ohio were considering shutting down or had already done so (Beaton, Colchin and Ma, 2020). An analysis by Candid projected a median figure of 7% closures nationally, with as much as 38% possible (Harold, 2020). The Nonprofit Finance Fund (2020) confirmed in its national survey that large percentages of nonprofits experienced major declines in every form of nonprofit revenue (earned income, gift income and government support) and that 60% said they faced long-term financial instability.

Still, as early as 2002 and even after the Great Recession of 2008–2009, nonprofits began to develop a reputation as a "resilient sector" (Salamon, 2002, 2012). There is evidence that the nonprofits sector managed to cope well in the Great Recession, though with considerable exposure and damage, especially for smaller organizations and certain subsectors (McCambridge and Dietz, 2020). Brown and her co-authors (2013) report that 5% of nonprofits with $50,000 or more of annual revenue closed during the 2008–2012 period compared to 4.2% of such closures in the previous four-year period, and 11.3% dipped below the $50,000 reporting threshold in 2008–2012 compared to 8.4% in the previous period. The authors also observe that "to survive the recession and reduced funding, many nonprofit organizations greatly reduced services, cut staff and took other drastic steps. Survival is not the equivalent to a robust sector that continues to deliver on the missions that charities pursue" (p.5). This is a very important point. Resilience is not simply about survival but also maintenance of viability, dynamism and effectiveness over time. It is well known that survival rate is only a limited indicator of resilience. Specifically, nonprofits' demise is notoriously difficult to measure because nonprofits can go dormant or continue to operate with diminished impact for many years while remaining technically alive. Even when the time for dissolution arrives, many nonprofits struggle with the procedures for going out of business; some linger indefinitely as "zombies" until stripped of tax exemptions and corporate status (Searing, 2020, p.361).

Pandemics and recessions are just two types of albeit terrible multifaceted crises. There are many other extant, often existential societal risks that can severely impact nonprofit organizations. Furthermore, nonprofit organization crises are not always easily connected to external circumstances. For example, organizations can be severely weakened in one set of circumstances and fail years later. A case in point was the Funding Exchange (FEX), a national network of social justice foundations created in 1979 by young idealistic philanthropists who sought to involve community activists in grant-making decisions. FEX was severely weakened by the Great Recession of 2008–2009 but continued to operate until 2013, when FEX's board announced the dissolution of the network and closure of its national office. FEX did not officially close its doors until 2018. The causes of FEX's demise are multiple and complex, including a scandal in one of its member foundations and tensions between members and the national office. However, the economic downturn of 2008 was a key contributing factor. The national office depended on returns from investments, tithes on members, fees from donor-advised funds and grants from large foundations, all of which were adversely impacted by the recession, leading to a 50% reduction in national office staff and a downward slide in the network's efficacy thereafter (Lurie, 2016).

Alternatively, nonprofits may suffer from internal weaknesses and/or an inability to adapt to change over a long period of time and then suddenly erupt into crisis. For example, the venerable Hull House in Chicago, founded by social pioneer Jane Addams in 1889, abruptly closed its doors in 2012 as a result of failures in internal governance that precluded its adaptation to new economic circumstances. The prominent social service agency FEGS in New York City experienced a similar fate and closed abruptly in 2016. Both of these large service organizations exhibited stress long before their closures, but leadership always believed there was more time to turn things around, until there was no time left. This book will examine both cases more closely in Chapter 11. Sometimes an organization contains the seeds of its own destruction, such as corrupt leadership. This was the case in the William Aramony scandal at United Way of America in the early 1990s (see Glaser, 1994) and the Bruce Ritter scandal at Covenant House in the late 1980s (see Redmond and Redmond, 1990).

These various instances demonstrate that even large established nonprofits are vulnerable to crisis, and that their recovery requires a capacity for resilience. The New York City Opera and the Cleveland Ballet were not so resilient and closed their doors in 2013 and 2016 respectively, after years of distinguished performance. The Denver Symphony closed in 1989 after 50 years of operation, ultimately to be reorganized as the Colorado Symphony Orchestra, which survives. United Way of America survives, but much weakened from its earlier prominence. The resilience of the Boy Scouts of America remains in the balance as it struggles with core issues of who can participate and who can lead their activities.

But should we really be alarmed by projections of nonprofit closures in the range of 5% to 10% in the pandemic or the Great Recession, or the spectacular demise of well-established nonprofits in recent years? After all, such an attrition rate is not far from the year-to-year experience of firms in the business sector in the United States, which has averaged 7.5% of firms exiting annually in recent years (Crane et al., 2021). And certainly there are spectacular examples of large business failures as well, such as Lehman Brothers, Enron and Sears. The difference, however, is at least two-fold. First, to a greater degree, competition and "creative destruction" is celebrated in the business sector as essential to productivity growth and innovation in the economy (Aghion, Antonin and Bunel, 2021), even if public policy often honors this more often in the breach. It is arguable that the nonprofit sector could also benefit from more competition and even creative destruction (see Chapter 9). Generally, however, our society expects nonprofits to cooperate and collaborate with one another in order to advance public interests and goals, rather than to engage in destructive rivalry (Harrison and Irvin, 2018). Second, as elaborated below, the special public goods character of nonprofit services calls for the preservation and building of institutional capital rather than allowing it to be regularly torn down and rebuilt as occurs in the business sector.

The nature of organizational risks and potential crises is explored further in Chapter 2. Here, suffice it to say that the risks are serious, manifold, intertwined and in many cases existential, and they confront nonprofits of every size, shape, mission and history. It is no exaggeration to say that potential risk should be a focal point of nonprofit management decision making, not just the subject of a playbook that is brought out when a crisis approaches or is already at hand. We argue in this book that nonprofits must become adept at both preparing in advance for potential risks, and deftly navigating catastrophic events when they do occur. Moreover, nonprofits must appreciate that failure to manage for resilience on an ongoing basis is in itself a risky course of action. But to achieve that perspective, there must be changes in the way that we as a society administer, support and regulate nonprofit organizations.

So, how are nonprofits handicapped by our present understandings of how best to steward these organizations? An important research paper by Aaron Horvath, Christof Brandtner and Walter W. Powell (2018) notes that "In the 1990s and early 2000s, nonprofits were increasingly urged to adopt managerial practices associated with businesses." These authors point out that some of these practices did indeed lead to improved organizational practice, especially the adoption of strategic planning, but also that "professionalization and the push for businesslike practices were experienced by many as a novel challenge to the heart and spirit of the sector." In any case, narrow interpretation of what it means to be businesslike as a nonprofit organization has certainly become problematic.

A seminal 2018 paper by George Mitchell and Thad Calabrese summarized several decades of scholarship and argued that nonprofits now live by four financial "proverbs" that are meant to ensure that they are trustworthy vehicles for carrying out their social missions and judiciously spending the economic resources with which they are entrusted. These proverbs are: "minimize overhead, diversify revenues, be lean, and avoid debt." The proverbs derive from a prevailing theory of nonprofit organizations first developed by Henry Hansmann (1980) that postulates that by observing a non-distribution-of-profits constraint, nonprofits build trust by minimizing the possibility that their resources will be misappropriated and wasted on self-enriching uses by nonprofit leaders. Hansmann argued that the non-distribution constraint enhances nonprofit efficiency by increasing the confidence of donors and clients who suffer an informational disadvantage (so-called information asymmetry) in the provision of the kinds of services that nonprofits typically provide, such as nursing care, day care, international relief, education, health care, and so on. In the presence of this nonprofit constraint, donors and clients are presumably more willing to consume and support such services than they would if providers were for-profit businesses. As a result, valued mission-focused services are provided that would not otherwise be provided, were it not for nonprofits. Hence the efficiency gains produced by nonprofits as a result of their trustworthiness.

The problem with the four proverbs, Mitchell and Calabrese argue, is that they are narrowly construed to reflect the demand for trustworthiness at the expense of efficiency and that they in fact constrain nonprofits from being efficient or effective in achieving their social missions. In particular, in the absence of direct measures of mission achievement (what some would call social impact), insistence on the four proverbs simply ties the hands of nonprofits without any evidence that they increase efficiency or effectiveness at all. Thus, it is not that the standard theory of nonprofits is wrong per se, but that it has led to a culture of measurement, accountability and regulation that is misguided and applied in a way that has made nonprofits fragile and less effective.

One can easily elaborate on the four proverbs to examine a variety of practices and constraints commonly applied to contemporary nonprofits. These include avoiding "profit" (that is, net positive revenues or annual surplus), limiting salaries and benefits of employees to levels seen as socially appropriate to charitable organizations, maintaining only minimal reserve or contingency funds, administering exceedingly tight budgets, overreliance on volunteers and other imperatives. The culture for this austere approach is pervasive. Ratings agencies such as the Better Business Bureau Wise Giving Alliance, Charity Navigator, Charity Watch and others offer guidelines to good practice that reflect these notions. Donors are advised to make their decisions on the basis of charity ratings; philanthropic foundations reinforce this viewpoint with grant-making policies that limit or disallow overheads or require matching funds; and governmental payment systems to nonprofits, in areas such as the social services, squeeze nonprofits with late payments and less than full-cost reimbursement for services rendered (Gronbjerg and Salamon, 2012). Indeed, government reimbursement for nonprofit contractors has been especially fraught. An Urban Institute study found that a third of sampled nonprofits reported that they had a "big problem" with payments that did not cover the full cost, and some 19% had a "big" problem with late payments. On average, nonprofits were owed more than $200,000 by their state contractors in 2013, compared to almost $85,000 by local government contractors and nearly $109,000 by federal government agencies (Pettijohn and Boris, 2013).

Academic and other programs of nonprofit management education and training also bear some responsibility for emphasizing myopic notions of efficiency. These include mantras of cost efficiency, and maximum social returns on investment, as if nonprofits were static economic institutions in a stable environment that are immune to crises and environmental change. Researchers have documented some of the dire results of these policies and practices, including a failure of nonprofits to maintain reserve funds (Calabrese, 2013) and a spiraling down of overhead rates resulting in a "nonprofit starvation cycle" that inhibits nonprofits from effectively maintaining themselves and addressing their missions (Lecy and Searing, 2015).

In this book we do not take issue with the need for trustworthiness or even efficiency in the deployment of nonprofit resources, so long as efficiency is properly characterized and measured. Efficiency requires that scarce resources be put to their highest valued uses (Young, Steinberg, Emanuele and Simmons, 2019), a proposition hard to argue with in principle. Economists distinguish between "productive" and "allocative" efficiency. Productive efficiency means that goods and services of a given quality are produced at the least cost. Allocative efficiency means that the right mixture of goods and services is produced in society. However, as noted below, these concepts must be nuanced to account for time horizons, the special character of nonprofit services and the presence of risk.

Efficiency, properly framed, is at odds with existing practices and ways of thinking, on three levels. First, as per Mitchell and Calabrese, current practice does not really reflect efficiency. Efficiency must be gauged by the impact or achievement of nonprofits' missions and goals compared to the cost of resources expended, not by adherence to arbitrary austerity measures or administrative or fundraising expense ratios.

Second, it is *long-term* efficiency over a period of years that really counts, not snapshot "efficiency" as reported on any given day or short period of time in some limited way. Long-term efficiency requires dealing with the dynamics of the environments in which nonprofits operate. In particular, nonprofit decision makers must take account of *risk*, and must manage risks in a manner that leaves them viable and able to address their missions under changing, often surprising circumstances. Prioritizing the short run short-changes the needs of future service recipients in comparison to those of today; moreover, it assumes that risks are known and require no special preparation for unplanned contingencies.

Third, efficiency in the management of nonprofit organizations must take into account the special public goods nature of nonprofit provision. Services provided by much of the nonprofit sector have the character of what economists have called "merit" and "option" goods. Option goods are those that must be available whenever people want or need them (Holtmann, 1983). That is, people value their *assured availability per se*. We want hospitals, social service agencies, emergency and rescue services, libraries, schools and colleges, orchestras, museums, foodbanks and shelters to be there whenever they are needed or desired, whether or not we regularly use them. This requires long-term maintenance and viability, not necessarily the best bargain at any given moment. Similarly, merit goods are those to which society as a whole (through its political process) attributes special importance and value beyond market value or other tabulations of individual benefits (Friedman, 2002): for example, the education of future generations or the preservation of cultural heritage. In all, nonprofits must think beyond simple efficiency measures of service delivery to assure that the merit and availability value of their services is accommodated.

The viewpoint that emerges when we reframe nonprofit management in terms of long-term efficiency, social value and reliability is *resilience*. We need to manage nonprofits for resilience, and a paradigm for resilience looks considerably different from the narrow efficiency and trustworthiness paradigm that now prevails.

In what ways? Nonprofit resilience management (NRM) would be a new way of thinking, ideally integrating several key elements:

- It would prepare nonprofits for the long run and for a variety of contingencies, both anticipated and unanticipated. As such, it would pose many "what if" questions, undertake scenario planning for likely and unlikely contingencies, and engage in a continuous process of strategic planning over time.
- It would focus on understanding the nature of risk and the strategies available for coping with different kinds of risk. It would be alert to the different kinds of risks associated with alternative social missions, and it would shape management of these risks accordingly. Importantly, it would recognize the riskiness of *failing* to prepare for catastrophic events.
- It would identify and operationalize a variety of ways for organizations to absorb shocks and adapt to new circumstances, including financial and economic as well as human resources and network-based strategies, as considered in various chapters of this book.
- It would incorporate measurement systems to detect threats and imminent emergencies, so as to avoid or better prepare for crises. And it would prescribe "stress tests" to determine if nonprofits are prepared and have the capacity to endure crisis situations.
- It would identify new opportunities stemming from crises that would enhance long-run performance and organizational resilience.
- It would recognize that nonprofit organizations vary widely with respect to their in-house analytic capabilities and management resources; hence the *NRM process must be tailored to the context and carried out within available resource limitations*. Essentially NRM is a way of thinking applicable, adaptable and important to nonprofits of every size and shape.

There is a counterargument, of course, that resilience, which some too-narrowly interpret as organizational survival, should not be a primary goal for nonprofit managers, and that sometimes organizations willingly risk demise and even succumb to Schumpeter's "creative destruction" (Aghion et al., 2021) in the interests of their missions and the improvement in societal welfare over time. Indeed, Horvath, Brandtner and Powell (2018) found that some of the organizations they studied in San Francisco in the 2008–2009 recession over-extended themselves in order to service the dire needs of their impoverished constituents. However, these researchers also found that the organizations in their sample that employed strategic planning, an instrument in the resilience toolkit, were more likely to survive. In this book, we take it as given that nonprofit leaders and managers want to preserve their organizations as a predicate to best serving their missions over the long term. That may not be the right judgment in every case, but we believe that it best serves as a guide for nonprofit organizational leadership. If creative destruction is to occur in the nonprofit sector, it is best left to external market forces and policy decisions of the society at large, not intentional demise or having individual organizations slip ineffectually into dormancy. Within that frame of reference, nonprofit managers and leaders should be taking their best shots at preparing for and navigating through future crises.

AN OPTIMISTIC OUTLOOK

If the foregoing focus on impending crises and nonprofit fragility seems unreasonably dour and pessimistic, that is not the intention. A new paradigm of nonprofit management based on resilience promises to lift the potentials for nonprofit organizational performance and the spirits of nonprofit leaders in several ways. First, managing for resilience will strengthen nonprofits so that their leaders and constituents can feel less threatened by potential disaster, less concerned about skating on thin ice, and better able to concentrate on the business of addressing their missions and serving their constituencies. Second, resiliency management strategy requires building in shock absorbers or margins for error – what we will call "organizational slack"; however, this slack would not be unproductive but would give organizations the flexibility in less turbulent times to experiment, innovate and plan for alternative futures, capacities they rarely have today. Third, when crises do occur, they often present new opportunities; a paradigm of resilience management will prepare nonprofit managers and leaders to identify such opportunities and exploit them in ways that improve their long-run performance and effectiveness. The recent crises that nonprofits in the United States and elsewhere have experienced over the past several decades have revealed the spirit and creativity with which nonprofits have responded to make the best of their circumstances.

A paradigm of managing for resilience would systematize what nonprofits have learned through crises so that they can be more productive in the future. In all, a paradigm of NRM would bolster the foundations of a forward-looking and optimistic sector.

BOOK PLAN

The next chapter delves more deeply into the nature of risks that nonprofits face, as well as the kinds of crises and contingencies for which they need to prepare. The chapter also considers the varieties of impact (economic and otherwise) these risks can have for nonprofit organizations and what policies and practices attach to different kinds of risk. An important message of this chapter is that an ostrich approach to risk is in itself highly risky.

Chapter 3 then probes the basic concept of organizational resilience, grounded in the notion of "organizational slack" as discussed in economics and organizational science, and broadened to embrace adaptability and flexibility as important capacities of healthy and growing nonprofits. This chapter makes an important distinction between navigating a crisis and preparing for (or preventing) one. Here we learn that resilience entails much more than falling back on financial safety measures and practices, but cuts across the entire spectrum of resource management practices and the building of healthy organizations.

Chapters 4 through 10 explore the various dimensions of organizational slack and resilience and how each yields a particular set of management strategies that can be pursued to achieve organizational resilience. These include "resilience strategies" connected to balance sheets, cost and revenue structures, human resource policies and practices, technologies by which an organization's services are produced, the organizational networks in which nonprofits are embedded, and entrepreneurial and leadership capacities.

In Chapter 11, we offer a broad perspective on "red flags" and "stress tests" tied to the multiple dimensions along which organizations can be vulnerable, monitored and strengthened for resilience. Finally, Chapter 12 brings all this together into a new paradigm of *managing nonprofits for resilience*. Fasten your seatbelts in preparation for navigating this journey.

SUMMARY

Many nonprofits are fragile and at risk of failing. The causes are manifold, including the financing and regulatory regimes in which they operate and the cultural norms they are expected to follow. At the same time, nonprofits operate in environments laden with potential catastrophic, even existential risks, as demonstrated by the 2008–2009 financial crisis, the COVID-19 pandemic and other recent events. These circumstances suggest that nonprofits must adopt a new paradigm of management based on resilience, not short-term and sometimes misguided indicators of efficiency. The chapters of this book offer a multifaceted approach to NRM that will alert nonprofits to impending crises and indicate how to better navigate and prepare for them. In preparing for the worst through resilience management, nonprofits can more confidently build a brighter future.

REFERENCES

Aghion, Philippe, Celine Antonin and Simon Bunel (2021). *The Power of Creative Destruction*. Cambridge, MA: Belknap Press.

Beaton, Erynn, Elizabeth Colchin and Yinglin Ma (2020). *Ohio Nonprofit COVID-19 Survey: A Report of Wave 2 Results*. Columbus, OH: Ohio State University, Philanthropy Ohio, Attorney General of the State of Ohio and Ohio Association of Nonprofit Organizations.

Brenan, Megan (2021). "Americans' Confidence in Major U.S. Institutions Dips." Gallup, July 14.

Brown, Melissa S., Brice McKeever, Nathan Dietz, Jeremy Koulish and Tom Pollak (2013). *The Impact of the Great Recession on the Number of Charities*. Washington, DC: Urban Institute, Center on Nonprofits and Philanthropy, July. http://nccs.urban .org.

Calabrese, Thad D. (2013). "Running on Empty: The Operating Reserves of U.S. Nonprofit Organizations." *Nonprofit Management and Leadership*, 23, 281–302.

Center for Effective Philanthropy (2021). *Persevering Through Crisis: The State of Nonprofits*. Cambridge, MA: Center for Effective Philanthropy.

Crane, Leland D., Ryan A. Decker, Aaron Flaaen, Adrian Hamins-Puertolas and Christopher Kurz (2021). "Business Exit During the COVID-19 Pandemic: Non-Traditional Measures in Historical Context," Finance and Economics Discussion Series 2020-089r1. Washington, DC: Board of Governors of the Federal Reserve System. https://doi.org/10.17016/FEDS.2020.089r1.

Faulk, Lewis, Mirae Kim, Teresa Derrick-Mills, Elizabeth Boris, Laura Tomasko, Nora Hakizimana, Tianyu Chen, Minjung Kim and Layla Nath (2021). *National Survey of Nonprofit Trends and Impacts*. Washington, DC: Urban Institute.

Friedman, Lee S. (2002). *The Microeconomics of Public Policy Analysis*. Princeton, NJ: Princeton University Press.

Glaser, John S. (1994). *The United Way Scandal*. New York, NY: John Wiley & Sons.

Gronbjerg, Kirsten A., and Lester M. Salamon (2012). "Devolution, Marketization, and the Changing Shape of Government-Nonprofit Relations," chapter 15 in Lester M. Salamon (ed.), *The State of Nonprofit America*, 2nd Edition. Washington, DC: Brookings Institution Press, pp.549–586.

Hansmann, Henry (1980). "The Role of Nonprofit Enterprise." *Yale Law Journal*, 89, 835–901.

Harold, Jacob (2020). "How Many Nonprofits Will Shut Their Doors?" Candid, July 15. https://blog.candid.org/post/how-many-nonprofits-will-shut-their-doors/.

Harrison, Teresa D., and Renee A. Irvin (2018). "Competition and Collaboration: When Are They Good for the Nonprofit Sector?," chapter 6 in Bruce A. Seaman and Dennis R. Young (eds), *Handbook of Research on Nonprofit Economics and*

Management, 2nd Edition. Cheltenham, UK and Northampton, MA: Edward Elgar Publishing, pp.118–131.

Holtmann, A.G. (1983). "A Theory of Non-Profit Firms." *Economica*, 50, 439–449.

Horvath, Aaron, Christof Brandtner and Walter W. Powell (2018). "Serve or Conserve: Mission, Strategy, and Multi-Level Nonprofit Change During the Great Recession." *Voluntas*, January 16. https://doi.org/10.1007/s11266-017-9948-8.

Independent Sector (2021). *Health of the U.S. Nonprofit Sector*. Washington, DC: Independent Sector.

Lecy, Jesse D., and Elizabeth A.M. Searing (2015). "Anatomy of the Nonprofit Starvation Cycle: An Analysis of Falling Overhead Ratios in the Nonprofit Sector." *Nonprofit and Voluntary Sector Quarterly*, 44, 539–563.

Lurie, Theodora (2016). *Change, Not Charity: The Story of the Funding Exchange*. New York, NY: Funding Exchange.

McCambridge, Ruth, and Nathan Dietz (2020). "Nonprofits in Recession: Winners and Losers." *Nonprofit Quarterly*, April 11. https://nonprofitquarterly.org/the-great -recession-nonprofit-winners-and-losers/.

Mitchell, George E., and Thad D. Calabrese (2018). "Proverbs of Financial Management." *American Review of Public Administration*, 49(6), 649–661.

National Intelligence Council (2021). *Global Trends 2040: A More Contested World*, NIC report 2021-02339. Washington, DC: National Intelligence Council. www.dni .gov/files/ODNI/documents/assessments/GlobalTrends_2040.pdf.

Nonprofit Finance Fund (2020). "COVID-19 Survey Results." March. https://nff.org/ covid-19-survey-results.

Pettijohn, Sarah L., and Elizabeth T. Boris (2013). "Contracts and Grants between Nonprofits and Government." Brief #03. Washington, DC: Urban Institute.

Redmond, R. H., and M. Redmond (1990). "The Paradoxes of Covenant House: Mythmaking & Lifesaving." *Commonweal*, 117(10), 311.

Salamon, Lester M. (2002). "The Resilient Sector: The State of Nonprofit America," chapter 1 in Lester M. Salamon (ed.), *The State of Nonprofit America*. Washington, DC: Brookings Institution Press, pp.3–61.

Salamon, Lester M. (2012). "The Resilient Sector: The Future of Nonprofit America," chapter 1 in Lester M. Salamon (ed.), *The State of Nonprofit America*, 2nd Edition. Washington, DC: Brookings Institution Press, pp.3–86.

Searing, Elizabeth A. (2020). "Life, Death, and Zombies: Revisiting Traditional Concepts of Nonprofit Demise." *Journal of Public and Nonprofit Affairs*, 6(3), 354–376.

Young, Dennis R., Richard Steinberg, Rosemarie Emanuele and Walter O. Simmons (2019). *Economics for Nonprofit Managers and Social Entrepreneurs*. Cheltenham, UK and Northampton, MA: Edward Elgar Publishing.

Cartoon 2   *We had another 100-year flood again this year!*

2.   Risk and the nature of crises

'Is it nearly over? In 2021 people have been yearning for something like stability. Even those who accepted that they would never get their old lives back
hoped for a new normal. Yet as 2022 draws near, it is time to face the world's
predictable unpredictability. The pattern for the rest of the 2020s is not the
familiar routine of the pre-covid years, but the turmoil and bewilderment of
the pandemic era. The new normal is already here.'

(The Economist, 2021)

Every year the *Economist* magazine makes end-of-year predictions about the
year to come. Here is what the editor said about its previous year's predictions
for 2021:

Well, we didn't see that coming. Like almost everyone else, we were blindsided by
the outbreak of COVID-19, the first cases of which were identified in December
2019. As well as causing death and hardship around the world, and the delay or can-
cellation of events large and small, one of the pandemic's less important side-effects
was to invalidate most predictions for 2020, including our own. (Standage, 2020,
p.74)

Mr. Standage should not feel so bad. At every level – individual, organizational, national and international – decision makers and prognosticators, year
after year, face almost innumerable, changeable, hard-to-anticipate risks.
Often, the best we can do is identify probable risks in broad terms, from trends
and developments that we already know about. The climate is changing,
technology is advancing, the demography of countries is shifting – in different
ways around the globe, the world and national economies have their ups and
downs, and nature contains surprises including new viruses, earthquakes and
perhaps even objects hurled our way from space. Human nature too is volatile
and especially consequential in jurisdictions or organizations with underlying
political tensions or unstable, possibly malevolent, leadership.

The only thing we can be really sure of is that "stuff will happen" and that
we need to be prepared. Many risks can be clearly identified and managed with
standard risk management strategies, including insurance and contingency

resources and plans. Others will seem to come out of nowhere, but these too require preparation. Consider the following general classifications:

- Ordinary, statistically predictable insurable risks: These include the risk of local fires, floods, accidents involving property loss or personal injury, or professional malpractice.

Such events occur with statistical regularity and are often insurable. Here the risk takers must determine what they are willing to pay for avoiding losses above some tolerable level, and insurers must calculate what they can offer in terms of policies that are profitable and competitive. So we have markets to manage this kind of risk (see Herman, Head, Jackson and Fogarty, 2004).

- Frog-in-boiling-water risk: Some risks are steadily growing but not necessarily on one's radar, and their consequences may be unclear and unfamiliar.

One cannot insure against climate change, globalization or technological obsolescence, though we know these are real and consequential. They just keep building until something happens, although we are not clear what that will be. The best we can do here is to learn as much as we can and then strategically plan for the future. This may help, but given human fallibility and limitations of knowledge, we need to have other weapons in our arsenal as well to cope with unanticipated consequences.

- Voluntary assumed risk associated with our conscious actions, choices and decisions in the ordinary course of business, including new ventures, appointing or electing new leaders, and other practices and policies.

Nonprofit managers and leaders make consequential decisions every day often with considerable uncertainty about outcomes. Examples include starting or terminating a service program, rehabbing or purchasing a new facility, renting versus buying office space, planning a fundraising event, installing a new management information system, engaging paid staff to complement or replace volunteers, choosing whether to charge for a new service or changing investments in an endowment.

Deliberate choices require decision makers to consider the consequences of alternative options, gather information and calculate possible outcomes as precisely as they can, and then make prudent choices. Prudence, however, does not mean minimizing risk or achieving certainty of outcome. Just as with private financial investments, tolerating some level of risk is usually necessary to achieve a desired return. Moreover, decision makers differ in their levels of "risk tolerance." Some decision makers (or organizations) are more risk-averse than others. While there may be ways to insure against terrible outcomes in some cases (for example, with high-deductible policies), such risk-taking is inherent in prudent decision making. Managing such risk requires that risk levels be taken carefully into account with appropriate calculations in the choice process (see Young, 2006).

• Catastrophic risks associated with unanticipated events such as pandemics, sudden economic downturns, political upheavals, scandals and calamitous natural disasters, and other unforeseen developments.

While in hindsight some of these kinds of events seem predictable, such prediction often requires searching for needles in haystacks. In retrospect we can often identify people who were sounding warnings about a coming pandemic, a stock market plunge, an incipient revolution or a terrorist attack. Part of risk management is thus to create a system of warning signals that will alert us to oncoming catastrophes of this sort. However, as Taleb (2010) argues, such "black swan" events usually catch us by surprise, with alarming consequences. This is the kind of risk on which we will largely focus in this book. The risk management strategy in this case is basically two-fold: (1) try to anticipate black swan possibilities through better planning and monitoring of the environment; and (2) be ready for surprises nonetheless. The COVID-19 pandemic is an example. There were warnings by far-sighted individuals such as Bill Gates (2015), but they generally went unheeded. Most people and organizations were surprised and were left unprotected. Alice Hill, a former member of the U.S. National Security Council, may have put it best: "We base all our choices about risk management on what's occurred in the past, and that is no longer a safe guide" (Flavelle, Plumer and Tabuchi, 2021).

An alternative perspective offered by Wucker (2016) is that many black swans are actually "gray rhinos"; that is, threats in plain sight that for one reason or another are willfully ignored until they bite us. Indeed, some analysts describe the COVID-19 pandemic as a gray rhino rather than a black swan event, given that virologists had been predicting such an outbreak for some time (Tooze, 2021). Psychologists describe such behavior as "normalcy bias," a human tendency to disbelieve or minimize threat warnings (Valentine and Smith, 2002), alternatively called the "ostrich effect." Why it is that members of the animal family are blamed for human failings is unclear and probably unfair to animals, but whether out of ignorance of an approaching black swan, or avoidance of an obvious gray rhino in the road, nonprofits can find themselves in the position of frogs in boiling water unless they prepare properly in advance.

Another human tendency, the opposite of normalcy bias, is of course, *over reaction* by obsessing on worst-case scenarios. This too is important to overcome in managing for resilience. In particular, decision making should

Table 2.1   Risk management strategies, adapted from Grace (2018)

	Low-severity	High-severity	Catastrophe
Low-probability	Cash flow	Insurance	Resilience
High-probability	Cash flow	Savings	Reinvention

be based on realistic assumptions about the likelihood and impact of adverse events. In the next section we sketch various categories of possible events in terms of their likelihoods and consequences. Here it becomes clear that planning for any singular catastrophic event is not judicious largely because such an event can be only vaguely defined and its probability is extremely low. However, anticipating that *some* serious untoward event of an undetermined nature will occur is the wise course of action.

THE NATURE OF RISK AND CATASTROPHE

Two principal parameters frame the seriousness of risk: the probability that something will happen and the consequences or impact if it does happen. With this in mind, we can adapt Martin Grace's (2018) four-cell matrix of loss financing options as shown in Table 2.1, expanded by an additional (fifth) column.

Grace's argument for the first column of "Low-severity" events is that management can handle these situations in the regular course of doing business. High-probability events should be planned for and included in operating budgets, and there should be enough "wiggle room" in those budgets for managing occasional low-probability, low-impact events as well.

The second column, of "High-severity" events, requires specific elements of risk management strategy. High-probability/high-severity events require explicitly setting aside savings to cover contingencies. For example, an orchestra can anticipate that its conductor or one of its principal players will become ill once in a while, and expensive replacements will have to be called in at a moment's notice. This is probably not an insurable expense, but it can be accommodated with a contingency fund designed to cover precisely this circumstance. Similarly, a nonprofit summer camp for children from low-income families can count on something going wrong with its physical plant (for example, its plumbing or power grid) every summer. This too may not be easily or cheaply insurable, but it can be covered by savings or reserve funds set aside for such contingencies. In these ways, savings can serve as emergency funds. Such funds might even be useful to protect against embezzlement, assuming someone other than the treasurer has the keys to the lockbox (!) – hopefully, though, that would be a low-probability event.

Insurance for risk can be helpful where the impact is severe and understood but the likelihood of an event is low. This is how insurance companies make money. They count on receiving your premium payment regularly but rarely having to pay out. Nonetheless, insurance provides comfort to organizational leaders for contingencies such as fires, floods, accidents that may injure clients and maybe even for criminal violations by leadership. While these are low-probability events, experience is sufficiently robust that their statistical likelihood can be reliably assessed and insured. Whether organizations buy such forms of insurance depends on their appetites for risk, the premium payments required, and their assessments of the probability and consequences of an event affecting their own situations (hopefully avoiding normalcy bias). An interesting example is directors' and officers' insurance for members of nonprofit governing boards. In a field with little exposure to external liability, such as an academic research association, organizations may decide to forego such insurance. In a field like nonprofit summer camps, purchasing such insurance may be wise to ensure that board members feel protected in the event of a serious accident affecting a camper.

Finally, a concern with insurance as a risk management strategy is what economists call "moral hazard"; that is, a tendency to become neglectful in following safe practices or in undertaking preventive measures given that, in the event of loss, insurance will cover some of the cost (Pearce, 1995). This effect increases the cost of insurance policies, possibly creating incentives for larger organizations to self-insure.

Consider the third column that we have added to Grace's table – catastrophic events, both high- and low-probability. The case of catastrophe and high-probability obviously spells big trouble. It is by construction beyond the possibility of insurance or internal absorption. This is where an organization needs to rethink what it is doing and either reinvent itself or close. It is not easy to think of examples here because most situations allow for some kind of preparation and amelioration strategy. An example might be a nonprofit that continues to try to rebuild in a flood plain when climate change suggests that those 100-year floods will now be recurring every 20 years, on average. Insurance becomes infeasible or too expensive, and internal resources cannot hope to recover the damages on a regular basis.

More relevant for our purposes here is the cell of catastrophic, low-probability events. These are the situations that we hope to avert by making our organizations more resilient. They are not insurable because we do not know exactly what they will be, their consequences and impacts may be unknown or not well understood, and they lack a statistical history that easily allows insurability. Moreover, the risks facing potentially insured populations in this category may be highly correlated with one another; that is, if one insured party is affected, it is highly likely that others would be as well, and all would file claims simultaneously, bankrupting the insurer. Lloyd's of London notwithstanding, insurance companies may classify the foregoing contingencies as "acts of God" beyond the scope of phenomena which they can accommodate. Moreover, their magnitude is beyond nonprofit organizations' expectations and normal capacities for dealing with emergencies. They are essentially the "black swan" events described by Taleb (2010):

> First, it is an *outlier*, as it lies outside the realm of regular expectations, because nothing in the past can convincingly point to its possibility. Second, it carries an extreme impact ... Third ... human nature makes us concoct explanations for its occurrence after the fact, making it explainable and predictable. (p.xxii; emphasis in original)

Recent experiences, such as the terrorist attacks on September 11, 2001, the meltdown of the finance industry in 2008–2009, the onset of the pandemic in 2020, and the storming of the U.S. Capitol in 2021, fit this description. We were blindsided by them, they have had enormous consequences, and we are still trying to understand and explain them. Certainly, they have had substantial and surprising impacts on the economy and the welfare of our society, including nonprofit organizations. In case of the COVID-19 pandemic, for example, losses of employment have run into the hundreds of millions worldwide, and lost income into the trillions of dollars (Tooze, 2021).

We will discuss such consequences in more depth below. First, let us consider further how likely it really is that such catastrophes will occur. After all, catastrophes are by definition low-probability events! Are they worth the trouble to worry about or divert our attention from everyday operations or conventional organizational development? The short answer is yes, they are worthy of our attention, and no, they do not require neglect of opportunities for regular organizational growth and development. While particular types of catastrophic events are indeed rare, the likelihood of some catastrophic occurrence, as we will explain, is not so rare. Thus, prudent investment in capacities to enhance organizational resilience should have expected returns commensurate with any other type of organizational investment. For small organizations, such investments would necessarily be modest. For larger, more complex organizations, greater levels of resilience-oriented expenditures would be prudent. A rule of thumb is that *an organization should invest to the point where it feels equally safe with and without additional investment.* This level will be different for every organization even if the likelihoods of catastrophe are the same. The rule derives from the micro-economic principle of "thinking at the margin" under which successive increments of investment in resilience would be compared to successive returns in safety, until the two have offset each other (see Young, Steinberg, Emanuele and Simmons, 2019).

Admittedly, estimating the returns from increased safety or reduced vulnerability is operationally challenging. However, this principle offers a way for managers to apply their best judgments to a critical, even existential issue in their own organizations.

THE LIKELIHOOD OF A LOW-PROBABILITY EVENT

In his 2020 book *The Precipice*, Toby Ord estimates the probability of various possible existential catastrophes occurring within the next 100 years. He defines existential risk as "a risk that threatens the destruction of humanity's long-term potential" (p.37). Clearly this is the most extreme consequence of a possible black swan event, resulting either in human extinction or an unrecoverable collapse of civilization. While nonprofit leaders would generally be concerned with catastrophic events of much less consequence, it is interesting to note the real, finite, if not frightening, possibility of even such world-ending events. Based on existing knowledge and research, Ord estimates two kinds of existential risk: natural risk and anthropogenic risk; that is, risk due to natural phenomena outside human control and risk resulting from human behavior, intentional or otherwise. In the natural risk category, Ord includes asteroid and comet strikes, supervolcanic eruptions and stellar explosions. He estimates a one in 10,000 chance of such an event in the next 100 years.

In the anthropogenic category, Ord includes nuclear war, unchecked climate change, pandemics, unaligned artificial intelligence (technology gone amok) and other possibilities. Astonishingly, Ord estimates the total anthropogenic risk at 1 in 6 over the next 100 years! As a result, he also assesses total existential risk at roughly 1 in 6 over the next century. In other words, we need to worry more about the consequences of human behavior than some cosmic event, despite what happened to the dinosaurs or the city of Pompeii.

While Ord strove to mobilize the best available information to make his estimates, his numbers remain highly uncertain and speculative, essentially an educated guess. Still, even if he is just in the ballpark, the fact that he is focusing only on extreme catastrophe should give us pause. A 1 in 10 estimate of existential risk over the next 100 years means that each year there is roughly a 1 in 1000 chance of an existential catastrophe. Considering the profound consequences, that is very frightening. Of course, one might argue that existential risk should be of little concern to organizational leaders. If something like that happens, there is not much use planning for resilience in a situation where there are no survivors or no functioning society within which to operate. However, Ord's analysis is relevant because it establishes lower limits. In particular, it does not account for non-existential yet catastrophic events which are liable to be much more common and localized. These are the events that managers and leaders need to be thinking about, even if they derive from some of the same sources, such as global pandemics, climate change or economic, political or technological disruptions. It is not clear how exactly to put a number on the likelihood of such events but we can start with Ord's order of magnitude in mind.

APPLYING THE RULES OF PROBABILITY

The probability of any particular catastrophic event (pandemic, recession, earthquake, leadership scandal, and so on) happening within a reasonably short, finite time frame and particular venue is small, although it increases as these time and venue limits are expanded. (Ord's numbers apply to the world as a whole, whereas we are interested in events that may impact a particular organization within some operational decision-making or planning time frame and place.) Still, given the *large number of possibilities of things that could happen*, the probability that *something* catastrophic will happen can be substantial, even within a limited context. For one thing, catastrophic events like pandemics and stock market collapses impact many organizations and jurisdictions all at once. Moreover, by definition, if something catastrophic does happen, the consequences will be very large.

Let us take the point of view of one organization making plans and decisions for a year's time. Following the rules of probability, we can divide the possibilities into two contingencies for that time period: Nothing will happen (N) and Something will happen (S). The probability of these two contingencies must add up to 1:

$$p(N) + p(S) = 1$$

Next we consider whether more than one catastrophe can occur within the period. Clearly this is possible, but let us first assume that potential catastrophes are "mutually exclusive of one another"; that is, the occurrence of one catastrophe precludes the occurrence of another in the same time period. If this assumption is reasonable then $p(S)$ may be estimated simply as the sum of the probabilities of all possible catastrophes:

$$p(S) = \text{SUM} (p_1 + p_2 + \ldots\ldots p_N)$$

where N is the number of different kinds of catastrophes that could possibly happen, and p_i is the probability that a catastrophe of type i will occur.

We can see that if the p_is are small (say 0.0001 on average) but N is large (say 1000), then $p(S)$ could be large; for example:

$p(S) = 1000 \times 0.0001 = 0.1$ or 10% that something will happen.

Is an estimate of 1000 different possible credible catastrophes reasonable? This is an exercise in imagination (think of Murphy's Law – what could possibly go wrong!), informed by the knowledge that we are constantly being surprised by what actually does occur from year to year. If N is just 100 then perhaps there is only a 1% chance of a disaster occurring, but if N is 10,000 a disaster of some kind is almost certain.

The foregoing estimate, however, must be corrected if catastrophes are not "mutually exclusive." For example, if a pandemic occurs, an asteroid could still hit in the same period of time. In this case we should deduct the probability of both a pandemic and an asteroid hit occurring, so as to not double-count the probability of both occurring. For two such events this is likely to be an extremely small number. For example, if a pandemic and an asteroid hit are so-called "independent events" (the occurrence of one not affecting the probability of the other's occurrence) then we would deduct the product of the probabilities of each event (say $0.0001 \times 0.00001 = 0.0000000001$). More generally, since there are N possible catastrophes, we should deduct the sum of the probabilities of any possible combination of catastrophes from our initial estimate of $p(S)$. Even with such a correction though, $p(S)$ can be a substantial number if the likelihood of any one event is not miniscule.

One way to see this is to picture a Venn diagram in which the probability of each catastrophe is a small circle within one large rectangle representing all possibilities, including the contingency that no catastrophe will occur (see Figure 2.1). Thus, the area of the rectangle corresponds to the probability value of 1 (something will either occur or not occur). The sum total area within all of the circles is the probability of some catastrophe occurring while the area inside the rectangle but outside any of the circles is the probability of a catastrophe not occurring. This depiction makes it clear that $p(S)$ is largest when all potential catastrophes are mutually exclusive – when none of the circles overlap as in Figure 2.1, and smallest when none are mutually exclusive of one another as in Figure 2.3 – that is, when all the circles completely overlap. (This would be as if all catastrophes combined into a single mega-event.) Figure 2.2 is the intermediate case where there is some, incomplete overlap of the circles. If we think that most catastrophes are not mutually exclusive, which is a reasonable possibility given the diversity of possible catastrophes, then *in the extreme*, $p(S)$ shrinks to the size of the circle of the single catastrophe with the largest probability (largest circle in Figure 2.3). In principle, this could be of some comfort. However, the degree to which potential catastrophes are indeed not mutually exclusive of one another and the probability of the most likely catastrophic event remain empirical questions. Moreover, taking comfort in *p(S)* being relatively small must be tempered by the realization that multiple catastrophes can more easily occur simultaneously if they are not mutually exclusive. That is, the probability of some catastrophic event will be lower in this case, but its consequences will be larger.

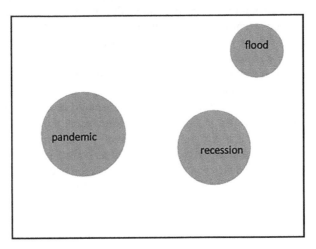

Figure 2.1   Mutually exclusive events

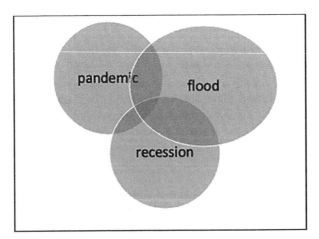

Figure 2.2   Non-mutually exclusive events

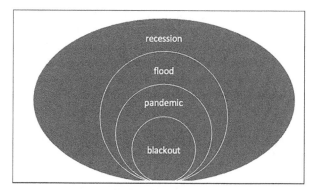

Figure 2.3   Completely non-exclusive (conjoint) events

Interdependent Catastrophic Events

Indeed, if catastrophes are not independent of one another, the onset of one is more likely to trigger another. That is, if one catastrophe happens, the probability of another can then be very high. For example, if the probability of a pandemic is 0.05 and the pandemic happens, then the probability of a recession *p(R/P)* might be as much as 0.9. In particular, using these numbers for illustration, and applying the rules of probability, we can calculate the probability of a recession, as follows:

$$p(R) = p(R/P)p(P) + p(R/NP)p(NP) = 0.9 \text{ x } 0.05 + 0.1 \text{ x } 0.95 = 0.14$$

which may be substantially greater than the probability of a recession if the two events were independent. That is, the probability of a recession might be only 0.07 were it not for the fact that a recession could be triggered by a pandemic.

This scenario also makes clear that the impact of something happening is likely to be more catastrophic than the singular impact of any one contingency. That is, the occurrence of a pandemic has its own consequences even if a recession does not occur, but is made worse by the fact that it is likely to trigger a recession. Indeed, analysts have coined the term "polycrisis" for situations where one catastrophe adds to the woes of another when it occurs in the same time frame, whether or not the events are independent (Tooze, 2021).

In short, *the probability of something happening – *p(S)* – is somewhere between the sum of the probabilities of individual catastrophes and the probability of the most likely catastrophe.* This is a broad range and requires empirical study to narrow it down. However, the estimate is certainly larger than the chance of any particular catastrophe occurring. Moreover, if some catastrophes are not independent of one another, then once some catastrophe has occurred the chance of another can become very substantial. For example, a pandemic increases the probability of a recession, a natural disaster increases the probability of an immigration crisis, an internet breach could increase the likelihood of a war, a famine could trigger a political crisis, and so on. In short, although the risk of a singular catastrophe is relatively low, leaders must be prepared for cascading crises whose consequences may be enormous.

IMPROVING PROBABILITY ESTIMATES WITH EXPERIENCE

The foregoing calculations were made with very rough numbers derived from a broad overview of world-threatening possibilities at a given point in time. A particular nonprofit organization may be able to make more precise estimates for its own circumstances. We begin here by making a fine distinction between "risk" and "uncertainty." We have characterized risk as an estimate of the probability that something of consequence occurs. We can characterize uncertainty as the fact that we are unclear about what the value of that probability actually is, though we can often specify a "distribution" of its likely values. And as we learn more about the risk, we may be able to narrow our estimate and make it more precise. Thus, in the above discussion we might start with a value of 1 in 100 for a catastrophic event in a given year based on general research but then update this information with experience in our own particular circumstances over time. This approach to risk estimation is based on Bayes' Law of probability (see Ash, 2008 for example).

Suppose we examine the United States from the viewpoint of a disaster management organization such as the Red Cross or the Salvation Army in, say, 1960. In each of the following decades through the 2010s we might notice that major unforeseen disasters seem to occur about two to three times per decade, depending on how you define "major disaster." In the 1970s we had legionnaires' disease and swine flu outbreaks and a near nuclear disaster at Three Mile Island. In the 1980s the OPEC (Organization of the Petroleum Exporting Countries) oil crisis resulted in "stagflation" of the economy – high inflation, slow growth and unemployment – and the *Exxon Valdez* oil spill occurred. The 1990s saw a major flooding of the Midwest by the Mississippi and Missouri rivers, and the Oklahoma City bombing. In the 2000s we experienced the 9/11 terrorist attack and the consequences of the Iraq War. The 2010s encompassed the Great Recession from the 2008–2009 collapse of the financial sector, as well as the *Deepwater Horizon* oil spill. In the 2020s we seem to be witnessing an acceleration of such events, already beginning with the pandemic, and social unrest following a contested presidential election and protests in connection with racism and police brutality. On the basis of this history, we would be wise to continually update our "prior" probability estimate of 0.01 to be closer to 0.02 by the end of this period. This process would continue to give weight to the longer history but also recognize that things may be changing or that we are simply becoming more certain of the actual value.

Moreover, this procedure would recognize that estimates for particular localities and organizations would differ because the nature of risks and the vulnerabilities to those risks differ from venue to venue. Just to consider natural disasters for instance, organizations in California would be more exposed to wildfires and earthquakes, those in Florida or the Gulf Coast to hurricanes, those in Georgia to ice storms and those in Hawaii to tsunamis.

There are three main takeaways from this discussion. First, that catastrophic risk will indeed vary from place to place and organization to organization. Second, that while the nature of those risks may vary in terms of the mix of possibilities, we really do not know what exactly is likely to occur in any given venue and time period. And third, and most importantly, the probability that *something* catastrophic will occur in any given year is nontrivial and requires preparation for resilience.

THE DIVERSITY OF CIRCUMSTANCES AND CONSEQUENCES

Catastrophes can impose a variety of losses, and these may vary from one type of organization to another and from one venue to another. Some organizations may find new opportunities in a catastrophe while others will suffer in various ways. Particularly relevant to nonprofits is the connection between mission and impact. Because nonprofits with different types of mission carry out their work in diverse ways and draw on different sources of support, they will suffer or gain differently as well.

Even within the narrow bounds of financial impact, nonprofits with different missions will fare differently. The benefits theory of nonprofit finance explains why this must be so (Young, 2017). In essence, nonprofits provide a wide variety of services which produce different combinations of public or group benefits and private or individual benefits. This means that nonprofits with different missions are likely to be financed in different ways. For example, public radio offers a public or collective benefit that is most amenable to support through charitable donations. Alternatively, a nonprofit day care center provides largely private benefits to children and their families, and is amenable to financing through fees. Nonprofits in other fields reflect their own combinations of public and private benefits and hence alternative income portfolios. Research universities, for example, depend on tuition fees as well as government grants and alumni donations, while museums and orchestras combine admission fees with gifts and memberships from art-loving donors.

As a result of this funding diversity, crises will have different financial impacts on different kinds of nonprofit organizations. As noted in Chapter 1, in the COVID-19 pandemic many organizations were forced to curtail in-person services, resulting in a particularly severe hit to earned revenues. Examples included theaters, museums, orchestras, universities and some churches. At the same time, those less dependent on fees, such as environmental organizations, public radio or human rights organizations, were less affected. Indeed, some organizations, such as foodbanks, found themselves facing increasing demand, stimulating greater donor support. In contrast, the Great Recession of 2008–2009 took a much greater toll on contributions without severely interrupting earned revenue. Hence, the financial impact of this crisis was substantially different from that of the pandemic.

Loss of income is just one of several impacts that nonprofits can suffer in a crisis. Here again the impacts will vary with the type of organization and its particular social mission. For example, an inner-city social service organization can face financial instability as a result of escalating costs if it is located in an area where rents are rising due to rapid gentrification. Organizations that are dependent on physical facilities such as group homes or residential treatment centers can experience significant losses of assets as a result of natural disasters that lead to fires and floods. Labor-intensive nonprofits such as hospitals, schools and mental health centers can experience critical labor shortages and burnout as a result of crises, such as in the pandemic, which increased demands on professional personnel while undermining their health. A particular aspect of the COVID-19 pandemic was its impact on the technologies through which nonprofits carry out their work. Organizations less dependent on on-site service delivery, such as research or advocacy nonprofits, more easily adapted to online operations, while those more dependent on face-to-face services, such as schools and museums, had to curtail operations and quickly adapt to online operation as best they could. Similarly, some social services organizations designed to help challenged individuals pivoted from on-site services to in-home care. Other organizations, such as YMCAs and Jewish Community Centers (JCCs), found ways to partially open up some of their operations (such as child care and fitness classes) within strict protocols to avoid virus transmission. In almost all cases, nonprofits became more dependent on the internet and online operation than they were before the pandemic.

Finally, crises can have important impacts on a nonprofit organization's reputation. In an externally driven crisis such as the COVID-19 pandemic, the Great Recession, or terrorist attacks as have occurred recently on churches, synagogues and mosques, how well the organization copes with the situation will either increase the confidence and support of its constituents or undermine

it. In an internally driven crisis, such as a leadership scandal, restoring confidence after a leadership change is critical to the long-term survival and health
of the organization.

Clearly the various impacts that an organization can experience in a crisis
often intersect. Loss of reputation will undermine sources of financial support
from donors and clients. Conversely, financial instability will affect reputation
and confidence in leadership. Staff burnout will undermine performance,
dampen confidence in leadership, undercut reputation and reduce capacity to
attract resources and control costs. Changes in technology will affect costs,
ability to raise resources, staff morale and ultimately performance, reputation
and financial stability.

The implications for managing these crisis impacts are two-fold. First, the
hazards associated with a crisis are likely to be manifold, not just financial or
staff-related. A full multidimensional assessment of the possible risks associated with a given crisis possibility is thus required for effective risk management. Second, risk management strategies themselves must be comprehensive
– more than just requiring an ample financial reserve fund or business plan.
Deeper questions must be addressed regarding how risks can be managed
in connection with technology, human resources, assets and liabilities, leadership, the supportive networks in which nonprofits are embedded and the
interplay of these various elements. Much of the rest of this book is devoted
to exploring how nonprofits can be more resilient along these multiple lines.

WHAT IF?

As we will discuss in the following chapters, there are multiple ways in which
nonprofit organizations can prepare themselves for crises and become more
resilient. However, the complex and varied nature of catastrophic events
makes it difficult to discern precisely what risks will manifest themselves
and what the impacts of a crisis will be. Thus, a more generalized approach
is required to protect against risk and manage through crises whose attributes
are hard to discern in advance. What is clear, however, is the multiplicity of
ways that nonprofits can be impacted. This means that nonprofit leaders must
ask themselves questions about these vulnerabilities and possible impacts, no
matter the nature of the crisis that may cause them. In Chapter 10 we go into
more detail about scenario planning, organizational stress tests and red flag
signals that can alert us to the imminence of crisis. Here we argue that leaders
would be well advised to regularly ask themselves, perhaps within the context
of a strategic planning regimen featuring a SWOT (Strengths, Weaknesses,
Opportunities and Threats) analysis (Dees, Emerson and Economy, 2002),

several "what if" (threat-related) questions that may help them to bolster their crisis-related resilience:

- What if one of our main revenue sources is cut off or severely squeezed? Earned revenue? Gifts and grants? Government funding? Volunteer services? What could we do in each case?
- What if our facility had to close down? What could we do?
- What if we were overwhelmed with new demands for service as a result of an external crisis? What could we do?
- What if a large number of our staff or those in critical positions were incapacitated? What could we do?
- What if there was a stock market crash that severely diminished our financial assets? What could we do?
- What if our current methods of delivering services were blocked or severely constrained? What if a supply chain problem arose that cut off critical inputs, such as medical supplies in a health care organization or gasoline for a meals-on-wheels program? What could we do?
- What if our leadership is incapacitated because of an accident or health issue? What could we do?
- What if we had a financial scandal? A personal leadership scandal? A scandal involving care of our clientele? What could we do?

In scenario planning, an organization can combine these impacts into hypothetical stories of how such impacts could emerge and manifest themselves. The key, however, is to anticipate these possible impacts in the first place. Recognition of the possibilities is the first step to wisdom in developing resilient organizations in the face of crisis-related risk affecting nonprofit organizations.

SUMMARY

Nonprofit organizations face a wide variety of risks and potential hazards. Some of these are statistically predictable and of manageable consequence, such as building fires, theft or accidents that harm staff or clients. Such risks are insurable and can be minimized by taking proper precautions. Other risks are voluntarily incurred in the course of organizational decision making, such as possible consequences of starting a new program, moving to a new location or building a new facility, hiring or firing a staff member, or investing an endowment in a mutual fund. In these decisions, nonprofits must take prudent, understandable risks, assessing the right combination of risk and reward in each case.

Nonprofits may face risks that can sneak up on them with major conse-quences, like frogs in boiling water. For example, a nonprofit may neglect its technological infrastructure, allowing its computers and communications systems to fall into disrepair or become obsolete, suddenly resulting in a system failure that cuts it off from its constituents. The obvious solution here is to be more vigilant and attentive to known hazards. Other risks may not be so predictable even with sufficient prudence, including so-called black swan risks which can blindside an organization with major consequences, such as a terrorist attack, tornado, sudden economic meltdown or banking crisis. Such low-probability, high-consequence, hard-to-anticipate risks require an organi-zation to be prepared and able to surmount a major disruption without knowing quite what to expect.

The laws of probability suggest that while any particular low-probability, high-consequence event is highly unlikely by definition, the probability of *some such event* occurring in a year or in five years may not be so unlikely. Moreover, catastrophic consequences can be linked like dominoes. If a pan-demic occurs, a recession is more likely, and a crisis of food security or social unrest may also become more likely. If a terrorist attack occurs, there is a good chance a community may go into lockdown, with ensuing economic disrup-tions, and so on. Certainly, the probabilities and consequences of disastrous events will vary across geographic locales and fields of service. Weather events, for example, such as tornadoes, hurricanes and wildfires, vary by region, though still serendipitous in their trajectories and impacts. Still, as a practical matter, managing for resilience requires attention to the possibilities and consequences of catastrophic events without knowing exactly what they might be. Moreover, the impacts of such events on nonprofits can be mani-fold, including major losses of assets or income, labor shortages, technology breakdowns and losses of reputation stemming from failures to cope with challenging circumstances.

One way for nonprofit leaders to anticipate and help prepare for low-probability, high-consequence events is to engage in a series of "what if" exercises that simulate alternative scenarios to answer for themselves, "What would we do if such-and-such happens?" More importantly, nonprofits must be ready to cope with circumstances that they cannot reasonably anticipate or prevent. How to do so is the subject of the next ten chapters.

REFERENCES

Ash, Robert B. (2008). *Basic Probability Theory*. Mineola, NY: Dover Publications.
Dees, J. Gregory, Jed Emerson and Peter Economy (2002). *Strategic Tools for Social Entrepreneurs*. New York, NY: John Wiley & Sons.

Flavelle, Christopher, Brad Plumer and Hiroko Tabuchi (2021). "Storms Exposing a Nation Primed for Catastrophe." *New York Times*, National Edition, February 21, p.1.

Gates, Bill (2015). "The Next Outbreak? We're Not Ready." TED Talk, April 3. www.ted.com/talks/bill_gates_the_next_outbreak_we_re_not_ready?language=en.

Grace, Martin F. (2018). "Nonprofits and the Value of Risk Management," chapter 11 in Bruce A. Seaman and Dennis R. Young (eds), *Handbook of Research on Nonprofit Economics and Management*, 2nd edition. Cheltenham, UK and Northampton, MA: Edward Elgar Publishing, pp.225–242.

Herman, Melanie L., George L. Head, Peggy M. Jackson and Toni E. Fogarty (2004). *Managing Risk in Nonprofit Organizations*. Hoboken, NJ: John Wiley & Sons.

Ord, Toby (2020). *The Precipice*. Paris: Hachette Books.

Pearce, David W. (ed.) (1995). "Moral Hazard." *The MIT Dictionary of Modern Economics*, Cambridge MA, MIT Press, p.291.

Standage, Tom (2020). "Ahem ... About Last Year – The World in 2021." *The Economist*, November, p.74.

Taleb, Nassim Nicholas (2010). *The Black Swan: The Impact of the Highly Improbable*. London: Random House.

The Economist (2021). "The New Normal." December 18–31, p.13.

Tooze, Adam (2021). *Shutdown: How Covid Shook the World's Economy*. New York, NY: Viking.

Valentine, Pamela V., and Thomas Edward Smith (2002). "Finding Something to Do: The Disaster Continuity Care Model." *Brief Treatment & Crisis Intervention*, 2(2), 183–196.

Wucker, Michele (2016). *The Gray Rhino*. New York, NY: St. Martin's Press.

Young, Dennis R. (ed.) (2006). *Wise Decision-Making in Uncertain Times*. New York, NY: Foundation Center.

Young, Dennis R. (2017). *Financing of Nonprofits and Other Social Enterprises*. Cheltenham, UK and Northampton, MA: Edward Elgar Publishing.

Young, Dennis R., Richard Steinberg, Rosemarie Emanuele and Walter O. Simmons (2019). "Economic Decision Making under Risk," chapter 10 in *Economics for Nonprofit Managers and Social Entrepreneurs*. Cheltenham, UK and Northampton, MA: Edward Elgar Publishing, pp.258–279.

Cartoon 3   *Resilience used to be in our mission statement, but it didn't last (sigh)*

3. Understanding organizational resilience

In classical micro-economic theory, business firms are assumed to minimize their costs in order to maximize their profits and outcompete other firms. While this assumption has been very useful in understanding how markets work and how interventions in markets such as regulation and taxation help to control monopolistic abuses of market power and enhance societal welfare, it was never a really good way of understanding the firms themselves. Indeed, this assumption has generated heated debate and controversy within the economics profession. In 1966 Leibenstein published a now famous paper in which he argued, with evidence, that many business firms did *not* minimize their costs. Leibenstein called this "X-inefficiency" and considered it a waste of valuable economic resources (although a useful concept in understanding actual firm behavior). If it was so wasteful, however, why were so many successful businesses behaving like this? Other economists began to study X-inefficiency, and they identified implicit value in the notion that so-called inefficient firms can draw on "slack" in response to extraordinary pressures. For example, in reviewing the research literature on X-inefficiency, Perelman (2011) observed that "[o]ne indication [of X-inefficiency] is that management seems to be able to ramp up efficiency quickly in response to the shock of new competition" (p.213). So the best strategy is not to minimize your current costs, but to consider possible futures and implement enough slack to help manage risk.

Indeed, in a world of uncertainty and change – and potentially catastrophic surprises – many business leaders and scholars have long understood that firms require a margin for error and the means to absorb shocks and cope with risk. As noted in Chapter 1, the same expectations about maximum efficiency and minimum cost have also been applied to nonprofits, except in this context it has been mandated by a culture and regulatory regime rather than a particular theory or behavioral model of nonprofit organizations.

In business and other realms, scholars have identified the notion of "organizational slack" as especially helpful in understanding the behavior and operation of organizations, profitmaking or otherwise. For example, Nobel Prize winner Herbert Simon (1997) recognized that realistically speaking, firms "satisfice" rather than optimize because they do not have the information, time and wherewithal to perfectly optimize their operations. As a result, "inefficiency" necessarily characterizes firms in the marketplace. Furthermore, scholars including Richard Cyert and James March ([1963] 2013) found that such "inefficiency" actually serves productive purposes in allowing firms to manage internal conflict, deal with uncertainty and encourage innovation.

March and Simon (1958) explain how organizational slack normally works:

> When resources are relatively unlimited, organizations need not resolve the relative merits of sub-group claims. Thus, these claims and rationalizations for them tend not to be challenged ... When resources are restricted and this slack is taken up, the relations among individual members and subgroups in the organization become more nearly a strictly competitive game. From this we predict that as resources are reduced (e.g., in a business recession for a business organization; after a legislative economy move in a governmental organization), intergroup conflict tends to increase. (p.126)

Reading between the lines here, slack saves an organization from enduring a constant state of tension and provides the wherewithal to tighten up when required by a crisis. In their path-breaking *Behavioral Theory of the Firm*, Cyert and March ([1963] 2013) further argue that slack is a stabilizing and adaptive organizational force that operates in good times and bad:

> Slack operates to stabilize the system in two ways: (1) by absorbing excess resources, it retards upward adjust of operations during relatively good times; (2) by providing a pool of emergency resources, it permits aspirations to be maintained (and achieved) during relatively bad times. (p.38)

This analysis suggests that organizations should have a plan for slack to determine how to store it in good times and dispense it in bad times. Like a personal savings account, extra income not targeted for immediate consumption can be saved, and later used as exigencies arise. In the case of organizations, however, slack can take many different forms in addition to monetary reserves. The distinguished political economist Albert O. Hirschman identified organizational slack as the lubricant that allows organizations (of any sort) to rebound from loss and distress. In Hirschman's (1970) theory of "exit, voice and loyalty," some of this slack takes the form of "loyalty" whereby a firm's customers and other supporters are willing to tolerate a certain level of performance deterioration before they decide to "exit" the organization and withdraw their support. In the absence of loyalty, or slack more generally, organizations would simply collapse in a storm and have no chance to recover.

SLACK AND GOLDILOCKS

Classical economists, management consultants and policymakers are not entirely wrong when they decry slack as a waste of resources. Clearly too much slack in an organization means that resources that could be employed to advance the organization's mission are going unused or being diverted to extraneous purposes. However, the interesting thing about the productive uses of slack as explained by Hirschman, Simon, Cyert and March is that *just the right amount of slack* is, paradoxically, "optimal." Too little slack and the organization collapses or underperforms; too much slack and the organization fails to achieve its potential. The trick in resilience management is to find the *right* levels and types of slack to assure organizational viability and vitality, while achieving the organization's best level of performance over the long term and in the face of risk and potential crises.

The concept of organizational slack is key to managing resilience for two reasons. First, such slack is the basic source of resilience, serving as a set of multifaceted shock absorbers to help an organization navigate through hard times. Second, such slack can take a variety of forms, translating into multiple ways for building resilience. Indeed, one of the forms that "slack" can take is "unrealized potential." For example, an organization might be exploring a collaboration or partnership with another organization that could yield economies of scale or scope (savings achieved by coordinating different kinds of services or operating at a larger scale; see Chapter 10). Having contingency plans along these lines in place, even if not immediately implemented, could serve as a reserve strategy that can be accelerated in a crisis. The same might be said of plans to pursue additional sources of revenue, develop new service technologies or realign the future workforce, as we will explore in later chapters.

To date, there has been relatively little research on the actual strategies and tactics employed by nonprofits to survive crises. However, a recent study of nonprofits in reaction to a prolonged state budget crisis in Illinois (Searing, Wiley and Young, 2021) reveals the multiple lines along which nonprofits draw on organizational slack to remain resilient. These authors identified five broad areas of activity on which nonprofits could draw to remain viable and protect themselves against deterioration and demise: Financial, including the use of credit and reserves, better management of cash flow, revenue diversification including identification of new sources, cost reduction and sale of assets; Human Resources, including pay and staffing reduction, initiatives to ameliorate staff burnout and substituting non-monetary for monetary rewards; Outreach, including increased advocacy and fundraising efforts, improved relations with external stakeholders and reliance on a parent organization; Programs and Services, including service or quality reductions, triage to protect core services, increased waiting lists, and coordination or consolidation of programs with other organizations; and Management and Leadership, including planning, improved relations with the governing board, initiatives with strategic external partners and even taking on personal debt. While these do not constitute an exhaustive list, they are indicative of many of the dimensions of organizational resilience strategy examined in the remaining chapters of this book. These lists also reflect the Goldilocks effect, as many of these tactics require a level of prior slack that can be utilized in a crisis as a way of remaining viable, though not so much that the organizations would be dysfunctional in ordinary times. As many of us remember from childhood, Goldilocks wanted things not to be too big or too small but just right. Thus, depletion of lines of credit or reserve funds, or sacrifices by staff, for example, can be successfully employed under crisis conditions but the "reserves" that they represent must eventually be restored, whether this means paying back the line of credit or rebuilding staff relationships and capacity after a stressful episode so that the organization is refreshed and ready for future challenges.

NETWORK RESILIENCE

One dimension of nonprofit organization resilience (and slack) that is included in the tactics that nonprofits have employed in crisis situations has to do with the fact that nonprofits are commonly enmeshed in a variety of external networks. As discussed by Koliba (2015), these networks include grants and contract networks, partnership networks, intergovernmental networks and advocacy networks. Moreover, as explained by Young and Faulk (2018), nonprofit organizations are very likely to belong to associations and federations of various kinds, ranging from corporate but decentralized entities such as the American Cancer Society, to franchise-like operations such as YMCAs, to bottom-up associations like the American Alliance of Museums. The importance of these networks raises two questions about nonprofit organizational resilience. First, what is their role in maintaining the resilience of their constituent organizations? Second, how do the networks themselves maintain their resilience? The first of these questions is a main focus of this book, as external relationships can be understood as a dimension of organizational slack and part of a safety net for individual organizations. The second question has more to do with how networks operate as whole systems. Here another branch of the resilience literature more concerned with eco-systems than individual organizations is informative.

In the environmental field, eco-system resilience, as explained by Walker and Salt (2006), is all about cycles of adaptation, growth and change, and the importance of "thresholds":

> Adaptive cycles describe how many systems behave over time, and how resilience varies according to the phase where the system lies. Thresholds represent transitions between alternate regimes. (p.93)

Applying the concept of thresholds to the stability of social enterprises, Young (2012) argued that the tensions intrinsic in these hybrid organizations between market success and the mandate to address a social mission require these organizations to maintain a delicate balance, which could be characterized as an unstable equilibrium. Hence, small changes in external conditions could cause these organizations to tip past their thresholds towards other, more stable equilibria either as business organizations or as explicit social purpose entities such as conventional nonprofits, or in a worst-case scenario they could tip towards organizational failure and demise.

The paradigm of thresholds and system equilibrium is relevant to the resilience of nonprofit networks because in a crisis the members of these networks may depend on one another for survival. If the system is stable, the network will survive and its members will be able to depend on it as a safety net. Indeed, the network could be strengthened in such a case. However, if a crisis stresses the network itself, its functionality may be called into question and both the viability of individual organizational members and the network itself may be threatened. The case of United Way of America is relevant here. The Aramony scandal in the 1990s (see Glaser, 1994) undermined the whole network of United Ways in the United States when its central node collapsed and the public reputation of all its members was brought into question. Some argue that the United Way network has never really recovered from this crisis, though it moved towards a fairly stable new equilibrium emphasizing greater local control.

LEARNING ORGANIZATIONS

One important characteristic of resilient organizations (and networks) is that they learn from their mistakes and experiences, and they are receptive to new ways of doing things. This idea was introduced in Cyert and March's ([1963] 2013) study of business firm behavior:

> a business organization is an adaptive institution. In short, the firm learns from its experience. (p.100)

Senge (2010) promoted what he called "learning organizations" which not only assess their performance and correct their errors, but also build "double-loop" learning into their culture and decision-making processes. Such learning systems not only correct mistakes but regularly re-examine organizational procedures and routines through which such decisions are made. The COVID-19 pandemic amply demonstrated the importance of organizational learning to build resilience, especially in adopting new technology. A report by Salesforce (2020) concluded that organizations already well versed in computer and modern communications technology were better prepared to navigate change in this era than others that were not so capable.

In his path-breaking 1986 book *Images of Organization*, Morgan explained that one way of understanding organizations was to compare them to brains. In doing so, Morgan had the following premonition:

> In the longer term, it is possible to see organizations becoming synonymous with their information systems ... This new technology creates a capacity for decentralizing the nature and control of work, allowing white collar workers engaged in related tasks to work in remote locations while being linked on a continuous basis through on-line information networks which maintain a fully integrated system ... The really big question raised by the brain metaphor, however, is whether organizations will also become more intelligent. (p.84)

The COVID-19 pandemic not only confirmed the vision of organizations moving to remote work to reduce the transmission of infection, but it demonstrated that organizations could work more effectively that way. In other words, there was slack in the technologies of many organizations, nonprofit and otherwise, making it likely that remote work would become a permanent part of organizational operations even when the pandemic was long past. Moreover, this double-loop learning will apply to other organizational strategies that have changed as a result of this crisis, including the ways that nonprofits raise and expend their resources, engage their workforces, exploit their assets and control their liabilities, and partner with other organizations in their environments. Organizational learning is thus a key factor in organizational resilience, if only to identify and engage various sources of organizational slack and maintain the viability of organizational networks.

LOOKING AHEAD

In the remainder of this book, we explore the requirements for building resilient nonprofit organizations. The ensuing chapters build on the two basic ideas introduced in this chapter – organizational slack and organizational learning. To signal ahead, we argue that (a) nonprofit organizations must identify and properly deploy their sources of slack so as to be ready for crisis situations, and (b) they must learn from their experiences and build systems that will allow them to prepare for the next crisis, whatever that may be. More specifically, the resilient organization will:

1. Develop and deploy its slack resources in the following ways:
    a. Arrange its balance sheet of assets and liabilities to provide appropriate cushions and contingency options for crisis situations;

    b. Adjust its cost structure for flexibility to allow achievement of greater efficiency in a crisis;

    c. Adapt its income structure to provide redundancy in the event of one or more lost income streams in a crisis;

    d. Develop and deploy alternative technologies that will allow the organization to continue operating if its principal ways of doing things are undermined in a crisis;

    e. Develop contingencies for engaging the workforce and covering payroll that can be implemented in a crisis without destroying long-term organizational capacity and mission effectiveness;

    f. Develop external relationships and networks that can serve as safety nets in a crisis;

2. Become a learning organization that can benefit from its experiences, both positive and negative, by:

    a. Developing appropriate red flag indicators and data systems that will warn of impending crises in advance;

    b. Carry out scenario planning to anticipate possible contingencies for which the organization should be prepared;

    c. Revisit experiences post-crisis and revise organizational plans and procedures accordingly;

    d. Develop an entrepreneurial mindset that will help the organization to identify new opportunities created by crises and make good use of underutilized assets.

SUMMARY

Organizational slack serves to buffer nonprofit organizations in times of crisis and should not be viewed as simply a manifestation of inefficiency. A resilient organization will seek to tune its levels of slack following the Goldilocks principle – enough to navigate crises but not so much as to undermine the organization's operational effectiveness. In a crisis a resilient organization will draw on its slack to maintain its viability; in better times it will rebuild its slack to comfortable levels and use it to lubricate its operation. A resilient organization is also a learning organization that measures its current state of wellbeing and the potential risks it faces, and learns from crises to improve the ways that it operates and the new opportunities it may be able to exploit. Nonprofit resilience strategy is multidimensional, involving scrutiny of several important dimensions of management where slack and learning can be examined, including balance sheets, cost structure, sources of income, technology, human resources, network relationships and data systems. Each of these is studied in the chapters to follow.

REFERENCES

Cyert, Richard M., and James G. March ([1963] 2013). *A Behavioral Theory of the Firm*. Mansfield, CT: Martino Publishing.

Glaser, John S. (1994). *The United Way Scandal*. New York, NY: John Wiley & Sons.

Hirschman, Albert O. (1970). *Exit, Voice and Loyalty*. Cambridge, MA: Harvard University Press.

Koliba, Christopher J. (2015). "Civil Society Organization Accountability within Governance Networks," chapter 5 in Jean-Louis Laville, Dennis R. Young and Philippe Eynaud (eds), *Civil Society, the Third Sector and Social Enterprise*. London: Routledge, pp.91–108.

Leibenstein, Harvey (1966). "Allocative Efficiency vs. X-Efficiency." *American Economic Review*, 56(3), 392–415.

March, James G., and Herbert A. Simon (1958). *Organizations*. Hoboken, NJ: John Wiley & Sons.

Morgan, Gareth (1986). *Images of Organization*. London: SAGE.

Perelman, Michael (2011). "Retrospectives: X-Efficiency." *Journal of Economic Perspectives*, 25(4), 211–222.

Salesforce (2020). *Nonprofit Trends Report*, 2nd Edition. www.salesforce.org/wp-content/uploads/2020/05/2nd-edition-nonprofit-trends-report-2020.pdf.

Searing, Elizabeth, Kimberly Wiley and Sarah Young (2021). "Resiliency Tactics during Financial Crisis: The Nonprofit Resiliency Framework." *Nonprofit Management and Leadership*, 32(2), 179–196.

Senge, Peter M. (2010). *The Fifth Discipline*. New York, NY: Currency Doubleday

Simon, Herbert A. (1997). *Administrative Behavior*, 4th Edition. New York, NY: Free Press.

Walker, Brian, and David Salt (2006). *Resilience Thinking*. Washington, DC: Island Press.

Young, Dennis R. (2012). "The State of Theory and Research on Social Enterprises," chapter 1 in Benjamin Gidron and Yeheskel Hasenfeld (eds), *Social Enterprises: An Organizational Perspective*. London: Palgrave Macmillan, pp.19–46.

Young, Dennis R., and Lewis Faulk (2018). "Franchises and Federations: The Economics of Multi-Site Nonprofit Organizations," chapter 15 in Bruce Seaman and Dennis R. Young (eds), *Handbook of Nonprofit Management and Economics*, 2nd Edition. Cheltenham, UK and Northampton, MA: Edward Elgar Publishing, pp.300–322.

Cartoon 4   I think we're OK. Our assets are liquid

4.   Assets, liabilities and resilience

BOX 4.1   PLAYHOUSE SQUARE

Playhouse Square (PHS) in Cleveland, Ohio is the second largest perform-ing arts center in the United States. It operates eleven theaters, promotes arts education and administers a downtown theater district encompassing businesses, entertainment venues and housing, intended to strengthen the regional economy. PHS closed its theaters in the COVID-19 pandemic with consequent loss of ticket revenues, and businesses in the theater dis-trict suffered as well. Nonetheless, PHS has weathered the pandemic in good shape, partly as a result of its preparation: a capital structure which includes substantial reserve funds, access to credit, endowments and net assets approximately equal to half of its total assets.

Research by accountants and economists over the past four decades on the financial health of nonprofit organizations is as close as we have come to developing a good understanding of the vulnerability of these organizations in a crisis. Although this research focuses largely on year-to-year financial strug-gles rather than catastrophic events that may threaten a nonprofit organization, it prioritizes survival and viability over efficiency per se, and it provides insights into how nonprofits can better prepare themselves for crisis situations. Much of this research focuses on a nonprofit's balance sheet of assets and liabilities, as well as associated financial statements such as cash flow and revenue and expense statements. These financial statements provide a known window into an organization's solvency and sustainability, a good place to start for examining strategies for resilience.

Assets and liabilities are the two main ingredients in an organization's balance sheet. Assets are, in Bowman's (2011) terms, "everything of value an organization owns" (p.17), while liabilities are "the value of all obligations an organization owes to other parties" (p.18). For long-lived tangible assets such as buildings and equipment, *depreciation* is commonly deducted from asset value (as measured by original cost) to account for the depletion or usage of those assets over time. Finally, the quantity called *net assets* is the difference between an organization's total assets and its total liabilities. In for-profit companies, this amount is the owner's equity; however, since a nonprofit does not have private owners, these are the assets left for the nonprofit's use after the debts have been paid.

PREDICTING FINANCIAL VULNERABILITY

In a seminal paper published in 1991, Howard Tuckman and Cyril Chang developed a way to categorize nonprofit organizations at risk of financial failure, defined as an inability to withstand a financial shock such as a sudden loss of revenue or a severe economic downturn. They used financial information and accounting ratios, a type of analysis very popular in the commercial sector but not frequently used in the nonprofit sector.

Tuckman and Chang identified four factors that put nonprofit organizations at risk of financial failure: low net assets, little or no (administrative) slack, a small surplus (operating) margin and few sources of revenue, all expressed in ratio form from financial statements. A series of follow-on studies by other researchers confirmed and elaborated on these factors by measuring their impact on an organization's economic demise in various ways, including whether they experienced multiple years of declining program expenses, net assets or revenues, or actual bankruptcy (Greenlee and Tuckman, 2007).

One reason that Tuckman and Chang's work is so important is that it actually identified organizational slack as a critical factor in promoting resilience. In their formulation, this was measured by administrative expenses divided by total revenue. An organization was considered healthier if this ratio was larger rather than smaller, meaning that there was more money being spent on administration per dollar of total expenses. This is a departure from the kind of efficiency thinking that has plagued nonprofits, as discussed in Chapter 1. Having administrative slack meant that, when hard times hit, there would be consolidation on the administrative side before service delivery was impacted. Tuckman and Chang's revenue-related risk factors will be addressed in Chapter 6. In this chapter we focus on the balance sheet concept of "net assets" which these authors took as a key signal of financial health.

CONCEPTS OF SOLVENCY

Traditionally, solvency is the line between owning and owing: Does the organization owe more to creditors than the assets it possesses? For commercial organizations or individual people, solvency is usually measured by comparing assets to liabilities; if the latter exceeds the former, then the entity is insolvent. However, the notion of solvency in nonprofits is complicated by a number of factors, including the multiple sources through which they earn funds, the restrictions that may be placed on the expenditure of these funds and the degree to which they attempt to earn profits on their services. In these ways, nonprofits differ from conventional businesses; thus, gauging solvency by the earning of net positive profits (over time) may be inappropriate. The more general notion of "net assets," reflecting the store of net value that a non-profit could conceivably tap in an emergency, comes closer to the mark.

Woods Bowman (2011) identifies three types of nonprofit insolvency, as follows:

- Balance sheet insolvency, or insolvency in liquidation. A nonprofit is balance sheet insolvent if its unrestricted net assets are negative because in this situation the organization would be unable to pay off all of its creditors if it was liquidated.
- Cash flow insolvency, or operational insolvency. If a nonprofit is balance sheet solvent but cannot pay its bills when due, it is cash flow insolvent.
- Capital inadequacy. According to Bowman: "Capital inadequacy comes into play when an organization is solvent on the first two criteria but everyone knows that it is struggling and some have given up on it" (p.30).

Additionally, the municipal bankruptcy of Detroit introduced another type of insolvency:

- Service insolvency. An entity is service insolvent if it is no longer able to meet the public goods and service needs it is obligated to provide by statute or contract (Abott and Singla, 2021).

All of these notions are relevant to resilience. If a nonprofit cannot ordinarily pay its bills on time, it is probably because it does not have sufficient financial reserves to draw on, which in turn would be needed to tide it over in a crisis. And if it suffers capital inadequacy it is tottering on the brink, crisis or not. The basic notion of balance sheet insolvency is probably the most conservative measure of financial vulnerability because it signals that even if the organization could sell off all its assets it could not cover all that it owes. This condition is probably more common among nonprofits than is generally acknowledged. One study of nonprofits in New York City (Roberts, Morris, MacIntosh and Millenson, 2016) estimated that fully 10% were balance sheet insolvent.

BOX 4.2   SALVATION ARMY

Philanthropist Joan Kroc bequeathed $1.5 billion to the Salvation Army (SA), which in 2004 was the largest single donation recorded (Wolverton, 2004). Kroc left specific instructions on how to use the money: half would fund buildings, while the other half would provide an endowment that *covered a portion of the operating costs of those buildings. Both parts of the gift were restricted, so in accepting it, the SA knew that a significant part of the operations would not be covered. The groundbreaking donation would require SA to boost other sources of income in order to comply with the terms of the gift.*

ASSET RESTRICTIONS AND LIQUIDITY

Cash flow insolvency is relevant to nonprofits because some of their assets may be *restricted* or *illiquid*. Restricted assets such as endowments or other established funds, or investment returns on such funds, may be legally designated for particular purposes and cannot be used for more general expenses. As a result, nonprofits can be "broke" while still having money in the bank. Restrictions, however, vary in their stringency. Governing boards may impose restrictions, such as designating some of the organization's assets as a quasi-endowment; however, they can reverse this decision, if necessary. In contrast, donors may also impose restrictions which cannot be reversed by the governing board or management without donor consent or court action.

On their face, such donor restrictions limit a nonprofit's resilience because they restrict an organization's flexibility to respond to crises. From the viewpoint of organizational management, it is always better to receive assets in unrestricted rather than restricted form, all else being equal. However, this conclusion comes with important caveats. If donors, for example, would not have provided the assets without restriction, it would usually be better to receive them with restrictions than not at all. Certainly this would be true of financial assets, but not necessarily nonfinancial, material assets. The latter, such as buildings and equipment or art or historical collections, could entail upkeep and maintenance costs that might outweigh their benefits. Famous cases such as the New-York Historical Society (Guthrie, 1996; see Box 4.3) or Joan Kroc's gift to the Salvation Army to build community centers (Wolverton, 2004) vividly illustrate this point. However, for financial gifts some would argue that restrictions on assets also serve as a kind of insurance against ultimate disaster, by forestalling unwise expenditures. Specifically, restrictions put a brake on management spending which in dire circumstances can often be overridden by the governing board, a legal petition or an appeal to the donor.

Another type of inflexible asset found on a nonprofit's balance sheet is one that is *illiquid* and cannot be easily sold to cover expenses. According to Bowman (2011), *liquidity* is "an ability to get cash quickly when it is needed" (p.35). The fact that an organization's flow of income over time may not match the time pattern of its expenses requires the organization to establish a "working cash fund" consisting of cash and securities that can be quickly converted to cash to pay bills when they are due. In addition, it is good practice for nonprofits to have an "operating reserve fund" to cover unexpected budget shortfalls or to seed projects that will eventually become self-supporting (Bowman, 2011, p.35). Although Bowman is referring to day-to-day circumstances where ups and downs occur as a matter of course, one can appreciate *how much more important* a reserve fund can be to protect against a serious crisis. Unfortunately, researchers find that relatively few nonprofits maintain reserve funds at adequate levels, or not at all (Calabrese, 2013). According to Bowman, Calabrese and Searing (2018), the median reporting nonprofit in the United States maintained an operating reserve of less than 20% of total assets, although this varies widely by subfield (p.103). The median nonprofit in only nine of 27 nonprofit subfields maintained a reserve fund equal to three to six months of expenses, clearly indicating widespread jeopardy in an extended crisis such as a pandemic or economic recession.

Other interesting variants of illiquid assets are so-called "privileged assets" (Bowman, Calabrese and Searing, 2018). These assets are the heart of a nonprofit organization's mission and can be sold only under dire circumstances. The latter authors give the example of Harvard Yard (the main square of Harvard University), but the issue is more general than that. In the COVID-19 pandemic, American museums eased their constraints on selling parts of their collections in order to cover expenses (Pogrebin and Small, 2021). The question of collections is complex: When should collections even be considered assets that could feasibly be liquidated or traded for other than replacement pieces for the collection? The issue is currently unresolved in the museum world, but it is obviously important from the viewpoint of resilience. One might, for example, consider classifying objects in a collection into various categories, such as: disposable, disposable only in dire circumstances and never disposable. Donors would obviously have a say in this. But it is an important issue for resilience. For example, if the New-York Historical Society had been able to quickly dispose of parts of its rapidly growing collection, including items of marginal historical importance, it might have raised significant revenues and simultaneously reduced its expenses, helping to keep it afloat (Guthrie, 1996).

BOX 4.3   THE NEW-YORK HISTORICAL SOCIETY

The New-York Historical Society (NYHS) had a rapidly growing endowment during the middle of the 20th century. Due to a matching increase in expenses, the Society opted to begin spending more than the prescribed minimum annual payout rate of 5% for many years. That minimum rate, which the law requires for private foundations, is designed to allow the

real value of an endowment to be maintained while assuring that founda-
tions do not hoard their funds. However, the rate also serves as a guide-
post for the level of payout to maintain an endowment in perpetuity. This
spending eventually caused the size of the endowment to erode to almost
nothing. If the NYHS had maintained the value of its endowment over
time by limiting its payout nearer to 5%, it would have continued to gen-
erate annual returns sufficient to weather the storms to which it almost
succumbed (Guthrie, 1996).

ENDOWMENTS

A sizable minority of nonprofits have endowed funds of varying sizes. Endowments are intended to preserve capital while providing, through appropriate investment of that capital, general operating income or income for specific purposes such as scholarships, salaries of employees with "endowed chairs" or maintaining a building. Indeed, a good practice for nonprofits receiving contributions for a new building is to insist on coupling gifts for a building with an endowment fund to maintain the facility over time. The controversy over Joan Kroc's gift to the Salvation Army for building new community centers centered on whether the gift included a sufficient additional endowment for maintaining these centers without imposing a new financial burden on the organization. Without such a fund, the organization would certainly be less resilient. As will be discussed in Chapter 5, one source of difficulty for nonprofits in a crisis is the presence of "fixed costs" which are ongoing whether or not associated revenue streams are interrupted. As noted in Chapter 6, an endowment provides a source of "fixed revenue" to offset such costs.

However, from a general resilience point of view, endowments can be problematic. As Hager observed in 2006, "[a] big endowment can open up your financial options, but it might also limit your ability to change with the times." An endowment whose returns are restricted to a particular purpose ties the hands of managers who would prefer flexibility in determining how to allocate funds to navigate a crisis. Thus, from a resilience perspective, a general endowment whose return is unrestricted is preferable to a restricted-purpose endowment. Moreover, endowments of any kind tie up a lot of capital relative to the income that they generate at any given time. In a crisis, a nonprofit manager would prefer having discretion over the entire corpus of an endowment, not just the investment returns. This is a good example of where slack (in this case, a surfeit of restricted assets) may not yield the agility that resilience requires.

This is not to say that the corpus of endowments is entirely inaccessible during a crisis. One option is to borrow against it if a lender is willing to recognize an endowment as a form of collateral. This can still be problematic for conventional loans because lenders know it can be legally difficult to access the endowment's corpus. In the COVID-19 pandemic, the Ford Foundation and other large foundations took another, more innovative approach by issuing tax-free bonds to provide extra assistance to struggling nonprofits, essentially borrowing money at low rates in the bond market while preserving the higher returns on the investments in their endowed funds (Ely and Calabrese, 2020). This enabled the foundations to respect the constraints on their endowments while leveraging their corpuses to make additional grants to help operating nonprofits in the crisis.

Another option is to invade endowment capital by appealing to donors to release conditions imposed on their endowment gifts or going to court to have them eased. Both of these are difficult strategies in the best of times, and in a crisis as well. But it is clearly possible for a nonprofit to overturn donor restrictions in the face of its own potential extinction.

Finally, there is a certain unique advantage to maintaining endowments for purposes of resilience. Like restricted funds in general, nonprofit managers are advised to keep their hands off them in normal times, thus preserving endowments for possible help in a crisis – unless of course the crisis itself undermines the endowment, as it tends to do in a severe economic recession or stock market crash. We can also see from the New-York Historical Society case that an organization can unwisely spend an endowment (and an organization) into trouble; thus, the payout constraint on endowment has merit as a means of preserving an organization's resilience.

In summary, nonprofits have good reasons to solicit and accept endowments, although their value in building resilience is mixed. Some donors prefer the perpetuity, recognition and control associated with contributing endowments, and nonprofits prefer having such endowments rather than not receiving such gifts at all. But while the limits on endowments undercut flexibility in allocating resources in a crisis, they also impose discipline that may preserve these resources for dire emergencies.

ASSET DIVERSIFICATION AND PARTITIONING

Just as financial investors seek to diversify their portfolios to reduce risk, nonprofit organizations can try to do the same. For example, one could balance physical assets such as land, buildings and equipment on the one hand with financial assets susceptible to stock market swings on the other. Such a strategy would make sense if the values of these two classes of assets were inversely correlated over time, so that losses of value in one tend to be compensated by gains in the other; having assets whose value changes are uncorrelated or inversely correlated would be useful for purposes of weathering crises. However, as Bowman, Calabrese and Searing (2018) observe, there is little evidence that nonprofits diversify their asset portfolios with risk in mind. This is likely because use of these assets in production of a nonprofit's services is the determining factor in explaining the proportions in which these inputs are engaged; in other words, if a nonprofit has a building, it is likely because the building is being used to deliver services and not because it would serve as a good hedge against stock market losses. Within each asset class, however, nonprofits would be wise to diversify their holdings as a matter of good practice, especially within endowment portfolios.

In contrast to diversification, some nonprofits actually partition their assets into separate organizational or legal categories that cannot be mixed, in order to minimize potential liability problems (Bowman, Calabrese and Searing, 2018). For example, if a nonprofit runs a profitmaking business it may choose to incorporate that business separately in order to limit any liability of the parent organization, should something go wrong. Provided the nonprofit maintains control (for example, by being the sole member of its social enterprise's limited liability company), this could provide liability protection while still diversifying the parent organization's asset portfolio.

LIABILITIES

If net assets are an indicator of an organization's resilience, then presumably a nonprofit should seek to avoid debt since debt reduces the value of this indicator. In fact, a large percentage of nonprofits do not incur substantial debt (see Yetman, 2007). Moreover, some theorists argue that debt is costly for nonprofits compared to other modes of mobilizing resources for capital projects (such as fundraising or accumulation of operating surpluses; see Jegers, 2018). One reason for this is that banks want collateral to back their loans, and nonprofit assets may not be easily secured or marketable should they be repossessed.

In terms of resilience, however, other considerations are important. In a crisis, it is helpful to have access to lending, and such access depends on having a strong credit history (see Tuckman, 1993). Thus, judicious borrowing over time may actually be good preparation for a crisis. One way for nonprofits to do this is to establish a working capital loan fund with a bank, to continually borrow and repay at modest levels, just to maintain the relationship. This is similar to the way individuals build their own personal creditworthiness: Having no debt can be a good thing but having no history of borrowing and repayment precludes building a strong credit rating to facilitate borrowing in a crisis situation. Having good relations with a financial institution can have other resilience-related implications as well. Notably, in the COVID-19 pandemic, nonprofits that maintained a strong relationship with a bank were better positioned to claim their shares of government relief funds because those funds were administered through banking institutions.

SOFT CAPITAL

Some important nonprofit organizational assets do not appear on financial balance sheets but are nonetheless extremely important with respect to building and maintaining resilience. These are three general types of soft capital: human capital, social capital and reputational (organizational) capital. Crises can undermine all of these three types of soft capital, but all are critical to preparation and survival of crisis situations.

As will be discussed in Chapter 8, there are various approaches to adjusting workforces in crisis situations, and choices among these can determine whether an organization survives and positions itself for recovery after the crisis. Fairness in the treatment of different groups of employees and volunteers, as well as effectiveness in redeploying workers in a manner that best maintains the organization's mission, are the critical factors in avoiding serious "depreciation" of this asset in the short run and rebuilding of the organization's human capital after it has experienced a crisis.

"Social capital" refers to the networks of relationships that the organization has developed with other organizations and groups in its supportive environment, including funding, supplier, and regulatory networks; consumer, client and community groups; and federations and associations to which the organization may belong. Some of these relationships may be strained in a crisis if the organization is unable to maintain services to its constituents or unable to secure previously available reciprocal benefits from its networks; other bonds may be strengthened by crises – for example, where federations or foundations provide various forms of assistance for their members. As Chapter 10 explains, the building and maintaining of social capital is an essential strategy for nonprofit organizational resilience.

"Reputational capital" refers to the level of regard in which an organization is held by its consumers, clients, funders and other constituents. By and large, nonprofits are built on trust and the reliability and quality with which they serve their stakeholders. When a crisis hits, its reputation for quality, reliability and integrity may be challenged. However, the manner in which an organization navigates a crisis can make or break its reputation. The experiences of major nonprofit organizations that have suffered serious reputational losses attest to this. For example, the American Red Cross after 9/11 and Oxfam in responding to storm devastation in Haiti have seriously undermined the effectiveness of these organizations as a result of reputational damage stemming from external crises. Moreover, other organizations that have suffered internal scandals that have thrown them into crisis; for example, Covenant House, United Way of America, Oxfam and the Boy Scouts of America have lost substantial reputational capital which they have struggled to recover. The lessons here are clear. Maintaining reputational capital is required to build resilience before a crisis, if only to facilitate access to financial and other resources; and crises themselves can seriously damage reputation if they are not effectively and ethically managed. What is less clear is whether reputational capital can easily protect a well-regarded organization in a crisis of its own making. High reputational capital requires meticulous maintenance if its dividends are not to be lost in a crisis.

Soft capital does not usually appear explicitly in financial statements, although it may when an organization is being valued for purposes of acquisition or merger. "Goodwill" is the accounting term for intangible assets that make up the difference between a nonprofit's "book value" and the value paid to acquire it. Even without formal valuation, however, these various forms of soft capital are essential, albeit intangible, components of the assets that underwrite a nonprofit organization's resilience.

UNDERUTILIZED ASSETS

Crises often lead to creative problem-solving, as we discuss in Chapter 9 on entrepreneurship and resilience. One important way for entrepreneurial managers and leaders to proceed in a crisis is to ask the question "How can we make better use of our assets?" Are some of these assets underutilized or could they be repurposed for more productive exploitation in a crisis situation? Typically, such assets are of two kinds – physical facilities and human resources. In the former case, nonprofits may discover that they can generate additional revenues by further use of their latent capacities – for example, offering space in museums, botanical gardens, churches and universities for private, after-hours events; or expanding their clientele base, such as providing day care services for students confined to on-line instruction while their parents work outside the home. These are markets that may have been created by a crisis (as the day care example suggests) or simply possibilities that have been overlooked until a crisis occurs. What makes such initiatives possible is the implicit slack in underutilized assets that can be put to use for revenue-generating purposes.

Nonprofits may also find aspects of their human capital to be underutilized, either because the crisis itself has restricted the deployment of workers in their regular duties, or because there are latent opportunities. Universities and arts institutions in particular have very talented professionals whose expertise can be offered to the public in the form of educational and performance programs and consultations that can generate new revenue streams. Even where such revenue possibilities are minimal, engaging the human capital of an organization for new initiatives in a crisis can have significant personal and organizational benefits. Continuing to engage employees and volunteers in such circumstances helps keep the workforce together for the longer run, reducing the considerable costs associated with rebuilding a workforce that has been depleted and demoralized. (See Chapter 8 for additional perspectives on workforce resilience.)

SUMMARY

The balance sheet of assets and liabilities provides important indicators of a nonprofit organization's financial health and prospective resilience in a crisis. As a gross measure, net assets reflect the reserve capacity of an organization to pay off its obligations and still remain in business in the worst of circumstances. However, many nuances apply. Restrictions on assets limit the ability of nonprofit leaders to allocate resources in a crisis situation. Thus, the liquidity of a nonprofit's assets is key, and the establishment of adequate reserve funds an important strategy for ensuring immediate application of liquid resources in response to crisis. In addition, although maintaining substantial debt can undermine an organization's resilience, the access to credit can be an important option for managing a crisis once it occurs. Maintaining a credit history is therefore a key component of a nonprofit's resilience strategy.

Endowed funds offer a mixed strategy for nonprofit resilience. The restrictions on use of endowment funds limit the utility of endowments as a staple of crisis strategy. However, endowments provide a restraining element to dissipation of a nonprofit's assets over time. As such, they may be self-preserving and potentially accessible in a serious crisis if restrictions can be overcome.

Financial balance sheets offer only a limited view of the total assets that a nonprofit organization may command. In particular, nonprofits have important sources of soft capital, including the human capital embodied in its labor force, the social capital in its external networks and relationships, and its reputational capital reflected in the esteem and trust in which it is held by its constituents and stakeholders. These soft assets (and liabilities if they turn negative) are essential and sometimes even more important to nonprofit resilience than financial assets. Critically, soft capital must be built in advance of a crisis in order to ensure resilience; moreover, crises must be managed in ways that preserve soft capital and even enhance it by demonstrating its crisis value.

Finally, assets can represent opportunity in a crisis, and underutilization of assets a source for building resilience. As elaborated further in Chapter 9, underutilized assets, including physical capacity, staff expertise and network relationships, can underwrite new entrepreneurial initiatives to navigate crises and build for the future. A broad conception of an organization's balance sheet, including both hard and soft assets and liabilities, can assist the formulation of a strong resilience strategy.

REFERENCES

Abott, Carolyn, and Akheil Singla (2021). "Service Solvency and Quality of Life After Municipal Bankruptcy." *Journal of Political Institutions and Political Economy*, 2(2), 249–280.

Bowman, Woods (2011). *Finance Fundamentals for Nonprofits*. Hoboken, NJ: John Wiley & Sons.

Bowman, Woods, Thad Calabrese and Elizabeth Searing (2018). "Asset Composition," chapter 5 in Bruce A. Seaman and Dennis R. Young (eds), *Handbook of Research on Nonprofit Economics and Management*. Cheltenham, UK and Northampton, MA: Edward Elgar Publishing, pp.97–117.

Calabrese, Thad D. (2013). "Running on Empty: The Operating Reserves of U.S. Nonprofit Organizations." *Nonprofit Management & Leadership*, 23(3), 281–302.

Ely, Todd, and Thad Calabrese (2020). "Borrowing for Impact: Leveraging Foundation Endowments with Debt." Brief, National Center on Nonprofit Enterprise, July 9. https://nationalcne.org/home/wp-content/uploads/2020/07/Borrowing-for-Impact -Leveraging-Foundation-Endowments-with-Debt.pdf.

Greenlee, Janet S., and Howard Tuckman (2007). "Financial Health," chapter 14 in Dennis R. Young (ed.), *Financing Nonprofits*. Lanham, MD: AltaMira Press, pp.315–335.

Guthrie, Kevin M. (1996). *The New-York Historical Society*. San Francisco, CA: Jossey-Bass.

Hager, Mark (2006). "Should Your Nonprofit Build an Endowment?" *NPQ*. https://nonprofitquarterly.org/should-your-nonprofit-build-an-endowment/.

Jegers, Marc (2018). "Capital Structure," chapter 4 in Bruce A. Seaman and Dennis R. Young (eds), *Handbook of Research on Nonprofit Economics and Management*. Cheltenham, UK and Northampton, MA: Edward Elgar Publishing, pp.87–96.

Pogrebin, Robin, and Zachary Small (2021). "Museums Are Divided Over Selling Their Art." *New York Times*, March 20, pp.C1, C4.

Roberts, Dylan, George Morris, John MacIntosh and Daniel Millenson (2016). *Risk Management for Nonprofits*. Oliver Wyman/Sea Change Capital Partners, March.

Tuckman, Howard P. (1993). "How and Why Nonprofit Organizations Obtain Capital," chapter 7 in David Hammack and Dennis R. Young (eds), *Nonprofit Organizations in a Market Economy*. San Francisco, CA: Jossey-Bass, pp.203–232.

Tuckman, Howard P., and Cyril F. Chang (1991). "A Methodology for Measuring the Financial Vulnerability of Charitable Nonprofit Organizations." *Nonprofit and Voluntary Sector Quarterly*, 20(4), 445–460.

Wolverton, Brad (2004). "Salvation Army Receives $1.5-Billion Donation from McDonald's Heiress." *Chronicle of Philanthropy*, February 5. www.philanthropy.com/article/salvation-army-receives-1-5-billion-donation-from-mcdonalds-heiress/.

Yetman, Robert J. (2007). "Borrowing and Debt," chapter 11 in Dennis R. Young (ed.), *Financing Nonprofits*. Lanham, MD: AltaMira Press, pp.243–268.

Cartoon 5   *This is not what I mean by economies of scope and scale!*

5.   Cost structure and resilience

Resilience in a crisis usually requires an organization to reduce and control its costs, especially when revenue flows are interrupted, as the YMCA of Metro Atlanta's experience illustrates. This calls for flexibility to adapt costs to current conditions. There are a number of ways that nonprofits can develop this flexibility. One is to adopt a cost structure that naturally expands and contracts with demand. This leads to trade-offs between so-called fixed versus variable costs. A second strategy is to identify potential efficiencies that can be exploited in a crisis, such as consolidating operations of different departments or indeed merging operations of multiple organizations, in order to exploit economies of scale and scope. A third strategy is to ensure that investments in administration and fundraising are sufficiently robust so that reserve and slack resources are available when a crisis hits. This chapter will explore the application and nuances of these strategies to fortify nonprofits' capacities to navigate the shocks associated with the onset of sudden and severe crisis situations.

BOX 5.2   APOLLO'S FIRE

Apollo's Fire (AF), established in 1992, is a highly successful internationally renowned baroque orchestra based in Cleveland, Ohio. Despite the interruption of in-person concerts in the COVID-19 pandemic, AF was able to maintain its economic health, due in part to its flexible cost structure, especially the avoidance of large fixed costs. Rather than maintain its own concert hall, AF performs in a variety of performance spaces in the region and abroad, including churches, arts centers, schools and museums. And rather than maintain a full permanent ensemble, AF draws on distinguished itinerant guest musicians, locally and globally as needed. This allows the organization to expand or contract capacity and engage specialized performers to meet demands of particular concerts without carrying large fixed costs.

FIXED AND VARIABLE COSTS

It seems intuitive that the costs associated with running an organization or a program within an organization would increase as more is produced and would decrease as less is produced. But things are more complicated than that, and we need to break costs down into components that have different relationships with output. In order to provide some good or service, an organization requires some infrastructure that must be in place before any production can take place at all. This infrastructure might consist of a core staff, a building and some basic office necessities like phones and computers. We call these *fixed costs* because once in place, they stay the same as production begins and output expands.

In addition, as output is produced we encounter *variable cost*s that do increase as output expands. A theater needs to pay its actors, ushers and maintenance staff for each performance; and supplies such as programs and cleaning materials must be purchased and utility bills paid for keeping the lights on and the water running. A day care center must employ care staff and materials for the children to use, as well as paying for utilities while programs are in session. Parenthetically, it is worth noting that some expense items, such as utilities, may entail both fixed and variable cost components; basic (fixed) utility charges may be incurred just to have water and electricity services in place, but these charges would increase with usage (the variable component).

As production is expanded the fixed cost gets spread over more units of output, tending to lower the "average cost" of production, so long as variable costs do not rise more quickly. Thus, an organization can pay its bills if it can charge a price or otherwise receive reimbursement to cover the average cost. However, if production is interrupted by a crisis, such payments may cease, and even if the organization shuts down its production it will be left having to pay for fixed costs. That is largely why many theaters, museums, schools, community centers and other nonprofit organizations faced large financial losses and were threatened with insolvency in the COVID-19 pandemic (see, for example, American Alliance of Museums, 2020; Harold, 2020; and Savitch-Lew, Dvorkin and Gallagher, 2020). Many of the organizations that financially suffered most are ones that have large fixed costs and few ways to cover them when they must close up for a substantial period of time.

One way to prepare for such a situation is to re-examine the organization's cost structure to determine if there are ways to substitute variable for fixed costs in a manner that does not seriously compromise the organization's capacity to carry out its mission. Often there is, but such substitution must be pre-emptive. By the time a crisis strikes it is usually too late and one is stuck with fixed costs – at least in the short term before major decisions can be made to restructure the organization's way of doing things. In Chapter 2 (and later in Chapter 11) we advise nonprofit managers to engage in "what if" scenario planning to anticipate the implications of low-probability, high-impact cata-strophic events. In this context, one should consider the implications of having to suspend output or reduce services. In such a scenario fixed costs must continue to paid while variable costs can be cut back. However, if measures can be taken to reduce fixed costs in advance, the financial impact of such an event can be mitigated.

The examples of Apollo's Fire and the YMCA of Metro Atlanta are instructive. In order to provide the desired high-quality musical performances consistent with its mission, Apollo's Fire clearly needed to incur certain fixed costs, including a paid music director and core musical ensemble that could define the repertoire and set the standards of play, as well as a basic administrative staff to keep the books, manage the operations, raise money and arrange concerts. Yet the organization also decided to *avoid* certain fixed costs often associated with orchestras, including a full-time salaried ensemble and a performance venue of its own. Instead, these cost components were engaged as *variable costs* incurred on a concert-by-concert basis through rental of avail-able facilities and contracting with musicians separately for each performance. By way of contrast, the YMCA had significant fixed costs, including facilities and salaried staff which required it to take drastic and disruptive action in adjusting its workforce and constricting usage but maintaining its facilities in the pandemic.

In a stable situation there are pros and cons to the strategy of favoring a cost structure emphasizing variable costs. In Apollo's Fire's case, having a fixed venue and permanent ensemble could make it easier to improve and maintain quality. And costs of negotiating venues and player contracts on a continual basis would be avoided. Alternatively, playing in a variety of places and engaging outstanding musicians from different places could also enrich the quality of performances. But the *resilience value* of Apollo's Fire's strategy lies in its flexibility. When a crisis hits the organization, it is not saddled with large fixed costs that it is unable to pay. As earlier noted, covering such fixed costs largely explains why orchestras, museums and many other arts organizations, and other facility-based nonprofits such as schools and community centers, often faced financial hardship and bankruptcy in the COVID-19 pandemic and other crises. Such was the case with the Atlanta YMCA, which was constrained by an intrinsic need to maintain its presence in multiple communities throughout the region.

One could argue that the variable cost strategy simply reflects the modern "gig economy" wherein businesses like Uber and Lyft replace classical taxi services and buses with on-call ride services. Rather than engaging salaried employees, these New Age businesses hire workers as independent contractors using their own vehicles, with consequent shifting of risk and cost burdens from companies to workers. Certainly, disenfranchisement of workers should be of concern to nonprofits, and workers should have a voice in the consideration of alternative cost structures.

Organizational survival and resilience require that the wisest choices be made between what costs should be fixed and which should be variable. Should the organization rent or buy its office and service facilities? Which of its functions need to be covered by permanent salaried employees and which can be as well performed by workers contracted for particular tasks and projects? For purposes of resilience planning, these choices should be explicitly identified and considered in light of their consequences for navigating crisis situations as well as their implications for service quality, mission impact and fairness to workers. The Atlanta YMCA had to make some very hard choices in reducing its permanent workforce in order to weather the crisis and reposition itself for the future. (Human resources issues associated with workforce flexibility strategies are considered further in Chapter 8.)

Finally, economists make a conceptual distinction between the *long run* and the *short run*. In the short run, there is little one can do about reducing fixed costs. In the longer term, one can adjust fixed costs – for example, move out of a larger into a smaller facility or vice versa, and expand or contract the size of permanent salaried staff. In this way, *all fixed costs become variable costs in the long run*. Resilience planning is a long-run business and an appropriate opportunity to revisit and adjust fixed costs to ensure that future crises can be successfully navigated.

BOX 5.3   OUR LADY OF THE WAYSIDE

Our Lady of the Wayside is a residential and community services organization for children and adults with developmental disabilities, headquartered in Avon, Ohio. It was established in the 1960s as a single residence. Beginning in the 1990s it grew to serve four counties with ninety homes as well as transportation and day programs for both residential and nonresidential clients. By 2022 Wayside was serving approximately 650 individuals with a paid staff of 590, and is the largest Ohio provider in the waiver program under which the state provides reimbursement for services to clients who qualify for a variety of services free of charge. According to CEO Terry Davis, growth has been achieved through diversification of programming and associated income sources by keeping clients' needs for leading a full life uppermost in mind. This has led Wayside to develop transportation services to take clients to their jobs and other places they need to go, and day programs to serve clients outside of residential care. During the COVID-19 pandemic Wayside had to pause its transportation and day programs, and sought new funding from federal and other sources to sustain its residential programming and infrastructure. Nonetheless, the organization successfully navigated the pandemic, increasing its total revenue from $33 million to $37 million between 2019 and 2021. Moreover, staff layoffs were avoided by redirecting transportation and day services employees into Wayside's residential homes to relieve residential staff of the additional burdens they faced in the pandemic. This included "COVID teams" organized and trained by the CEO and overseen by the Nursing Department to provide round-the-clock care in the residences where needed. Davis attributes Wayside's resilience to its size, resulting from decades-long growth, taking advantage of economies of scale and scope to improve the efficiency and flexibility of operations and ensure the quality and comprehensiveness of services to clients.

ECONOMIES OF SCALE AND SCOPE

The scale at which an organization produces a given service generally affects its unit cost. For example, if we measure the output of a school by the number of students it teaches, it is liable to be more expensive at a small scale of a few students and more economical as a larger number of students is accommodated. Assuming maintenance of uniform quality as scale is increased, unit cost will decrease up to some level of class size and is then likely to level off or perhaps increase at larger scale as more resources are needed to maintain quality, overcome congestion issues and cope with more complex logistics. Such a situation would reflect a U-shaped cost curve wherein "economies of scale" are achieved in some mid-range. It is also possible for some services that such economies continue to be achieved at larger and larger scale. For example, the unit cost of an advocacy operation, measured by the number of prospective constituents reached with a given message, might continue to decrease indefinitely as the outreach network grows without significant commitment of additional resources.

A major determinant of economies of scale is fixed cost. If a certain infrastructure is needed just to be in business but that infrastructure need not grow much to accommodate more and more usage, and if variable costs per unit of output stay about the same or even decline at larger scale, then economies of scale can be reaped indefinitely by increasing output. In this case, average cost begins to approximate variable cost, with fixed costs per unit declining in relative weight as it gets averaged over more output. A good example is the ticketing function in the arts. Small individual arts organizations cannot run their ticketing operations as cheaply as a comprehensive arts center that handles ticketing for multiple organizations at once.

A popular notion in nonprofit management and especially in the social enterprise field is the presumed imperative of "going to scale," which suggests that all ventures and programs should grow to some larger size in order to have maximum impact. This idea must be qualified by an understanding of economies of scale. In the short term, programs can be expanded to lower their average costs within the constraint of its fixed costs. But economies of scale are really achieved over the long term, when fixed costs can be adjusted to achieve lowest possible unit costs. However, if economies of scale are achieved by increasing fixed costs, a price may be paid in terms of resilience. Apollo's Fire might be able to offer more concerts at lower unit cost by securing its own concert hall or expanding its core ensemble, but it would be saddled with those additional costs if a crisis undercut demand and cut off box-office revenue. Indeed, this is what happened to the Atlanta YMCA. In any case, "going to scale" should *not* be taken as a clarion call. Rather, scaling up should be carefully considered to determine both the scale at which an enterprise operates most efficiently and the risks associated with concomitant fixed costs. For example, although Our Lady of the Wayside has clearly followed a productive growth strategy over several decades, it paused its expansion of residential homes in the pandemic because of the risk of overextending its ability to cover the costs of new infrastructure.

Similar to economies of scale, so-called "economies of scope" are achieved by combining the production of two or more different services so that they contribute to one another's output, reducing unit costs of the combination. Such economies might be achieved either because there are aspects of production (including joint costs as discussed below) that can be shared and jointly administered or because the alternative services actually contribute to each other's effectiveness. A classic example is the twinning of preventative and treatment programming in social services organizations. If problems such as substance abuse or homelessness can be prevented or detected in advance of their worst manifestation, then treatment becomes either unnecessary or less costly. If these functions are separately provided by different organizations there may be barriers and costs that undermine coordination or joint planning, whereas in a single organization these may be overcome by easier communication and logistics. Similarly, Our Lady of the Wayside's diversification of its programming into transportation and day services reflects the synergies and cost savings associated with the interplay of these programs with its residential program and its desire to achieve a more comprehensive and effective way to serve its clients in a holistic manner.

What do economies of scale and scope have specifically to do with organizational resilience and crises? One can argue that ideally if such potential economies exist, they should be exploited in the ordinary course of business, allowing organizations to operate more effectively and efficiently day to day (see Harrison and Irvin, 2018). While this is true in principle, the barriers to realizing prospective economies of scale and scope in ordinary times can be formidable. Economies of scale require capital investment for expansion. However, nonprofits are often limited in their options to finance capital projects, relying on donations and borrowing, but generally without access to equity markets. Often the best path to scale economies is through partnerships with specialized organizations such as performing arts centers or other joint endeavors that serve multiple providers. Or, if an industry is fragmented into multiple, small independent organizations, such as churches or community centers, merging some of these organizations together could be sensible if not easily achieved. Similarly, economies of scope may require merging of different organizations offering complementary services to a given target population. Achieving those economies can also face daunting challenges in ordinary times.

Crises, however, offer opportunities to exploit economies of scale and scope under duress, if organizations are prepared to act when the time is right. This requires foresight and groundwork. The potentials for unrealized economies of scale and scope may be thought of as a form of organizational slack but there must be a plan in place to absorb that slack in a crisis situation. Part of any organization's strategic plan should be the identification of opportunities to achieve these benefits should a crisis occur. Certain fields of nonprofit activity have illustrated this potential – for example, substantial numbers of mergers of social service organizations over decades in the later 20th and early 21st centuries. Organizations such as the Jewish Board of Family and Children's Services in New York City (https://jewishboard.org/) or the Centers for Families and Children in Cleveland (https://thecentersohio.org/) are agglomerations of several smaller independent social services agencies over time, exploiting economies of both scale and scope. More recently, in the COVID-19 pandemic various small colleges have similarly been absorbed by larger and more financially healthy colleges and universities; for example, Pine Manor College by Boston College (Larkin, 2020).

It is understandable that smaller and more vulnerable nonprofits would want to protect their autonomy and independence, and in normal times perhaps they should. But their integrity and resilience also requires that they plan for contingencies, in part by identifying options to partner and perhaps merge with other institutions in their fields. As well, larger and less vulnerable institutions should explore how they can work with their more fragile counterparts to exploit potential scale and scope economies in order to build mutual resilience.

Finally, it is important to note that economies of scale and scope may be differentially relevant to nonprofit organizations in different stages of their development over time. As discussed by finance scholars Greenlee and Tuckman (2007), nonprofits commonly evolve through several life cycle stages, which these authors identified as: Birth, Stabilization, Growth, Diversification and Closedown. During the Growth stage organizations will seek to take advantage of potential economies of scale, and during Diversification they will look for economies of scope. In the Stabilization and Closedown stages, organizations may seek help, including from potential partners which they may find in growing and diversifying organizations. In a crisis period, when resilience really matters, potential scale and scope economies can be realized, to the mutual benefit of nonprofits in all stages of their development – hopefully to avoid the final stages of Closedown.

SHARED COSTS

When a nonprofit organization engages in more than one kind of activity, its activities may share certain common costs. These can be costs of administering the organization as a whole rather than any particular program (often called "indirect" costs), or costs associated with particular programs that serve multiple purposes, such as fund development and community relations (often called "joint" costs). To illustrate the former, a college may offer both an undergraduate program and a lecture program for the community. These programs may share the indirect costs of financial administration, libraries, computer infrastructure and physical plant. Usually, some accounting formula or method is used to determine how much of such costs to allocate to each service; for example, proportions of floor space used or relative numbers of student or faculty hours. These formulas are needed for accounting and reporting purposes and can have important real economic effects. For example, they may influence internal budgeting or personnel allocations for the alternative services, or levels of reimbursement by funders.

To illustrate the latter (joint costs), consider fundraising. If fundraising is simply considered a profitmaking endeavor (to maximize net revenue for the organization), then all of its cost should be assigned to that activity. If, instead, fundraising events such as dinners, 5 kilometer runs or golf tournaments are aimed at educating the community about the cause or building relations with potential volunteers, then some of the costs of "fundraising" events can be assigned to other functions than fund development because the event is also accomplishing other goals. Indeed, in a function such as fundraising the allocation of joint costs may influence the scale of operations. In particular, a larger scale for an event may be chosen even if costs exceed fundraising revenue. Nonprofits sometimes get themselves into trouble by setting fundraising goals too high and then spending more on them than they take in. That might be justified if they are clear about allocating joint costs elsewhere, or if events are viewed as investments with expected payoffs in the future. But sometimes such arguments are just excuses for poor planning. Overextension of fundraising campaigns can be costly, and they can make nonprofits less resilient.

In a crisis, the juggling of accounting estimates (assigning indirect or joint costs) may seem like rearranging deck chairs on the *Titanic*. But again, contingency planning can be helpful if there are revenue implications associated with cost reporting. There are several possibilities here. First, many nonprofit services may be reimbursed by government on a cost-related basis. Within permitted limits, if cost reporting can be shifted towards services associated with higher reimbursement rates or more reliable revenue streams, this could provide the organization with an economic cushion in a crisis.

Similarly, nonprofits with commercial income ventures are subject to Unrelated Business Income Tax (UBIT). This tax is based on reported profits. If, within acceptable accounting practices, joint costs can be shifted towards unrelated commercial services, then the profits on which UBIT is calculated will be lower. It is no surprise, therefore, that despite the widespread practice of commercial revenue generation by nonprofits, precious little unrelated business tax is actually paid (Brody, 2009). Finally, if the nonprofit is organized internally into independent "cost centers" associated with alternative services for which different prices are charged, shifting joint costs towards those services for which demand is relatively "price inelastic" (that is, will not experience drops in demand proportionate to price increases) can be helpful. In this case, prices can more easily be raised to cover costs without decreasing revenues, a potentially useful option in a crisis situation.

In summary, within legal, professional and ethical limits, accounting for shared (indirect and joint) costs may offer one limited avenue of resilience for some nonprofits in anticipation of a crisis situation. Like taxpayers in the general economy, nonprofits should consider claiming all benefits to which they are entitled, or at least have this option ready in their resilience toolkits.

ADMINISTRATIVE COSTS AND OVERHEAD

As noted earlier in this book, nonprofits face pressure from donors, regulatory bodies and rating agencies to keep their administrative and fundraising costs low. Much of this pressure is misguided and puts nonprofits in financial jeopardy, especially in a crisis. In the context of resilience and crisis management, there are two basic concerns: First, nonprofits are made fragile by not pursuing their best economic interests in ordinary times. Second, nonprofits will not have sufficient administrative infrastructure in place to maintain their efforts when a crisis hits.

The limits recommended or imposed on nonprofits' administrative and fundraising costs are generally framed in terms of *averages*: Nonprofits should limit fundraising cost to a certain percentage of their gross receipts and limit their administrative costs to a certain percentage of their total expenses. Norms like 10% or 15% are suggested and nonprofits compete for donations by extolling their low percentages compared to other organizations. Rating agencies bless "lower-overhead" organizations in their reports.

While intended to reduce administrative bloat and increase resources devoted to mission-related programming, these "standards" can be destructive on both scores, especially in a crisis situation. One man's administrative "bloat" is another's sensible organizational infrastructure and slack. And the level of investment in infrastructure will fall short of that which could have produced the largest net return on fundraising and the largest possible mission-related programming impact.

Economists frame the determination of the "optimal" level of administrative and fundraising cost using the concept of *thinking at the margin* (see Young, Steinberg, Emanuele and Simmons, 2019). This is easiest to illustrate in the case of fundraising costs. Thinking at the margin in this context means increasing fundraising expenditure dollar after dollar until the last dollar spent is just offset by another dollar raised. The likelihood is that each dollar spent up to this limit will yield more than a dollar in return, so that maximum net dollars will be raised by spending up to this limit. Moreover, this limit is likely to substantially exceed that which would be raised under some imposed maximum on the average cost of raising these funds. A simple numerical example will help.

Suppose an organization spends $1000 on fundraising and that yields $10,000 in return, and suppose 10% is the recommended limit on fundraising cost. The net yield at this level is $9000. Now suppose the organization spends another $1000 which then yields an additional $8000, or $7000 in net contributions. The net yield has increased to $16,000 but the fundraising ratio is increased to 11% ($2000/$18,000). Does it make sense for the organization to adhere to a 10% norm? Certainly not, as that would mean losing $7,000 in net revenue. Incidentally, as suggested earlier, the same logic applies in reverse. Sometimes nonprofits throw in the kitchen sink to achieve some arbitrary fundraising goal, even if additional dollars spent yield less than a dollar in return (that is, a net loss).

The situation is made a bit more complex by the fact that promulgation of arbitrary fundraising and overhead standards can (and do) influence donors. Indeed, the system can be self-defeating as more stringent standards dampen donor enthusiasm for funding worthy but more costly programming, and nonprofits race to the bottom in their administrative investments (Lecy and Searing, 2015). However, the solution is not to limit overhead costs but rather to change the system and to reeducate donors and the general public not to pursue the faulty logic of arbitrary average standards.

The foregoing argument about fundraising costs can be extended to general limits imposed on administrative costs. Administrative costs underwrite the capacity of a nonprofit organization to achieve its mission-related goals. If an additional investment in administrative capacity allows an organization to achieve additional impact of greater value than that increment of administrative cost, that increment should be expended. And that logic should be extended with further rounds of incremental expenditure until additional administrative cost is just offset by the value of the corresponding incremental impact. The result will be the maximum net social impact that the organization can achieve. The corresponding level of administrative cost is unlikely to conform to some arbitrary guideline such 10% or 15% of total cost, but will be determined by the intrinsic nature of the service being provided. Granted, it is often difficult to estimate the dollar value of additional increments of mission impact without a formal benefit–cost analysis (Young et al., 2019); however, the logic of this process, using management's best judgments and estimates, should prevail over arbitrary externally imposed or recommended guidelines. Nor would it necessarily be wise to gear one's administrative cost levels to those of peer organizations that provide similar services. For one thing, few organizations offer precisely similar services or pursue identical social missions. For another, unless peer organizations pursue the forgoing logic themselves, a nonprofit will be unreasonably constricted in its administrative capacity. Third, even the foregoing marginal analysis logic can be too stringent if it does not include consideration of the role of administrative capacity in building resilience so that a nonprofit can ensure its ability to deliver social impact under threatening circumstances.

Indeed, the issue of investment in administrative and fundraising infrastructure is made more urgent in the context of building organizational resilience. Underinvestment is more likely to result in fragile underfunded organizations with fewer reserves, which are more vulnerable to crisis (Calabrese, 2013). Moreover, in the midst of a crisis, such organizations will not have the administrative capacity to seek the additional resources they need to survive.

It could be argued that maintaining some slack administrative capacity itself entails "opportunity costs" because such resources might be devoted to expanding services or otherwise promoting mission-related activity. After all, if crisis events are "rare," why be so conservative? First, as Chapter 2 explains, crises are not so rare as to be ignored, especially given potentially devastating consequences. Second, as noted throughout this book, planning for slack must be prudent. Bloated administration is to be avoided, but so is an administrative infrastructure that is overstretched and incapable of a crisis response. Moreover, as examined in other chapters, slack can be put to good use in ordinary times. For example, in Chapter 8 we argue that slack in the workforce can be productively engaged in organizational learning and improvement in normal times, and ready to respond when the organization is threatened.

SUMMARY

Several aspects of a nonprofit organization's cost structure can influence its resilience in a crisis. Large fixed costs can result in unpaid bills when revenue streams tied to output are constricted. And constrictions on investment in administrative and fundraising infrastructure can make organizations fragile in normal times and lacking the capacity to raise sufficient funds or address other needs in an emergency situation. These concerns call for examining the balance between fixed and variable costs, and investment in administrative and fundraising capacity, as elements of a robust resilience management and planning strategy.

Additionally, nonprofits can examine their potentials to exploit economies of scale and scope in the services they provide, and the manner in which they account for joint costs of providing multiple services. Such investigations can lead to contingency plans to achieve greater efficiency or more robust revenue streams to protect the organization over the long term.

REFERENCES

American Alliance of Museums (2020). "National Snapshot of COVID-19 Impact on United States Museums (October 2020)." www.aam-us.org/2020/11/17/national-snapshot-of-covid-19/.

Brody, Evelyn (2009). "Business Activities of Nonprofit Organizations," chapter 4 in Joseph J. Cordes and C. Eugene Steuerle (eds), *Nonprofits & Business*. Washington, DC: Urban Institute Press, pp.83–127.

Calabrese, Thad D. (2013). "Running on Empty: The Operating Reserves of U.S. Nonprofit Organizations." *Nonprofit Management and Leadership*, 23, 281–302.

Greenlee, Janet S., and Howard Tuckman (2007). "Financial Health," chapter 14 in Dennis R. Young (ed.), *Financing Nonprofits*. Lanham, MD: AltaMira Press, pp.315–335.

Harold, Jacob (2020). "How Many Nonprofits Will Shut Their Doors?" Candid, July 15. https://blog.candid.org/post/how-many-nonprofits-will-shut-their-doors/.

Harrison, Teresa D., and Renee A. Irvin (2018). "Competition and Collaboration: When Are They Good for the Nonprofit Sector?," chapter 6 in Bruce A. Seaman and Dennis R. Young (eds), *Handbook of Research on Nonprofit Economics and Management*, 2nd Edition. Cheltenham, UK and Northampton, MA: Edward Elgar Publishing, pp.118–131.

Larkin, Max (2020). "Under Financial Stress, Pine Manor College to Join Boston College." WBUR/Edify. www.wbur.org/edify/2020/05/13/pine-manor-acquisition.

Lecy, Jesse D., and Elizabeth A.M. Searing (2015). "Anatomy of the Nonprofit Starvation Cycle: An Analysis of Falling Overhead Ratios in the Nonprofit Sector." *Nonprofit and Voluntary Sector Quarterly*, 44, 539–563.

Savitch-Lew, Abigail, Eli Dvorkin and Laird Gallagher (2020). "Art in the Time of Coronavirus: NYC's Small Arts Organizations Fighting for Survival." Center for the Future. https://nycfuture.org/research/art-in-the-time-of-coronavirus.

Young, Dennis R., Richard Steinberg, Rosemarie Emanuele and Walter O. Simmons (2019). *Economics for Nonprofit Managers and Social Entrepreneurs*. Cheltenham, UK and Northampton, MA: Edward Elgar Publishing.

Cartoon 6   Maybe we're going too far with diversification!

6. Income portfolios and resilience

A special feature of nonprofit organizations is their capacity to access a variety of distinctly different sources of income, including sales or earned income, charitable contributions, government funding, gifts-in-kind (including volunteer labor) and returns on invested funds. Nonprofits do so in many different combinations that reflect their missions and the particular services they offer. For example, in the United States, environmental organizations rely mostly on charitable contributions, health care organizations depend largely on earned income, and arts and culture organizations are roughly equally dependent on both these sources. Education nonprofits lean towards fees (tuitions) with a substantial reliance on contributions, while human service organizations favor fees and government support, with a substantial level of charitable support as well. Within these very broad categories of nonprofits there is substantial variation, reflecting a variety of social missions and programs. Overall, these differential patterns of nonprofit income "portfolio" composition are explained by the *benefits theory of nonprofit finance*, which stipulates that the sources of finance track the public/private nature of the services that a nonprofit organization provides (see Young, 2017).

For purposes of resilience management, a major takeaway from benefits theory is that every nonprofit has its own natural base of finance in terms of the combinations of different sources that it is able to cultivate. Resilience management requires that an organization position itself to take full advantage of its potential. With this perspective to anchor the analysis, other aspects of income resilience strategy can be considered. First, diversification of income sources is itself a risk management strategy that can protect nonprofits and allow them to be more resilient in a crisis. Second, certain "fixed" kinds of income can protect against losses associated with unanticipated shutdowns in operations. In this chapter we will discuss sources of fixed income that are invariant to changes in output, as well as "semi-fixed" types of income that are slow to change when a shutdown or slowdown occurs. These strategies reflect the fact that crises can affect the sources of nonprofit income in several different ways, and that these impacts can be difficult to predict or anticipate. Thus, income resilience strategies must help compensate for a variety of potential income stream losses.

HOW CRISES CAN IMPACT DIFFERENT SOURCES OF INCOME

The COVID-19 pandemic took a particular toll on nonprofits' earned income because it required theaters, schools, museums, social enterprises like Edwin's and other venues for on-site service to shut down and therefore lose paying customers or use-related reimbursements. Income from charitable contributions and general government support was less affected; indeed, governments and foundations themselves worked to provide extra assistance to nonprofits in financial jeopardy. And the stock market continued to soar, yielding additional investment income to nonprofits with substantial endowments (including grant-making foundations). Moreover, certain nonprofits, such as hospitals and foodbanks, experienced increasing demand during the pandemic, although the impact of these increases is complex. Hospitals had to forego more remunerative services such as elective surgeries in order to respond to the COVID-19 emergency. Foodbanks received increased in-kind and financial contributions from donors, allowing them to service increasing numbers of people who became unemployed or were otherwise hurt financially by the pandemic.

In contrast, the 2008–2009 Great Recession in the United States took a broad toll of the economy, including the stock market. Thus, charitable contributions were hit severely, but nonprofits could continue to operate and generate earned income. If anything, the recession increased the imperative for nonprofits to find additional sources of earned income to compensate for slower charitable giving and investment income losses.

Another important consideration, noted by Chang, Tuckman and Chikoto-Schultz (2018), is that crises can change the character of nonprofit revenue streams themselves. For example, after the 9/11 terrorist attacks:

> donors shifted their dollars towards charities that met 9/11 needs and away from those that had other missions. The impact was severe ... some nonprofits proposed and funded projects designed to fill homeland security needs, and still others altered existing programs to fit them within a framework that made them attractive to donors with this interest. In a sense, anti-terrorism became a new source of funds. (p.30)

The latter experience is also, of course, another example of new opportunities manifested in a crisis situation, to which nonprofits must be alert. Another such example is the rise of crowdsourcing, facilitated by the explosive growth of social media and internet communications. Crowdsourcing may be particularly sensitive to emergency appeals for funding if the crisis entails compelling humanitarian needs which a nonprofit is well positioned to address. As Chang, Tuckman and Chikoto-Schultz (2018) duly note, this is more likely to be a short-term source of help rather than a sustaining revenue stream. Still, crowdsourcing can be a useful resilience strategy for nonprofits, similar to other crafted emergency appeals responsive to the circumstances. For example, in the COVID-19 pandemic, foodbanks have been successful in stimulating donations, given rising community needs, and member-focused organizations such as Jewish Community Centers or museums have been able to appeal to their members for extra short-term help to sustain the institutions to which they are already committed. Clearly, disaster response organizations such as the Red Cross, CARE and Doctors Without Borders are well versed in funding by emergency appeal. While these various efforts rely mostly on more traditional means of solicitation, crowdsourcing can extend this strategy as a supplementary effort to reach wider communities of interest.

Philanthropy often plays a special role both in responding to crisis situations and in affecting the longer-term resilience of grantees. Individual donors as well as major foundations commonly make extra efforts to help when disasters strike, such as in the COVID-19 pandemic (Candid, 2021). However, phil-anthropic practices can also make nonprofit organizations more fragile and vulnerable to crises in the longer term. For example, nonprofits can become dependent on the ongoing largesse of specific major donors. When such donors fail to renew their commitments, nonprofits can be left with significant gaps in their income streams if they have failed to anticipate this contingency and have not planned for it. This can easily happen if organizational resources are concentrated on fulfilling the implementation and reporting requirements of a large gift, to the neglect of cultivating other sources of support. Moreover, it can be difficult to identify alternative donors willing to provide support for a previous donor's commitment, as the emphasis of major donors tends to be on funding new initiatives that can be associated with their own identities. In addition, donors may create conditions that undermine a recipient organization's economic stability. Often, they are chary of funding "overhead" in favor of direct programming leaving nonprofits thin on administrative infrastructure and unable to maintain slack resources that donors may view as wasteful. Further, donors may impose additional cost obligations that they leave unfunded. A classic case is the funding of new buildings or facilities that obligate an organization to raise additional funds to complete a project as well as to provide for its maintenance over time. In such cases, nonprofits must be wise to look gift horses in the mouth so as not to threaten their long-run stability or to distort their mission-focus. The gift Joan Kroc gave to the Salvation Army for the construction of new community centers around the United States is one example where questions were raised about the sufficiency of funding for building and maintenance as well as the impact of the gift on the mission-focus of local Salvation Army chapters (Wikipedia, 2022).

Other streams of income can also help in a crisis but may increase nonprofits' vulnerability in the long term. For example, government funding was instrumental in rescuing many nonprofits from bankruptcy or mass layoffs in the COVID-19 pandemic (National Council of Nonprofits, 2022). However, these funds are temporary, and dependence on them could undermine an organization's stability in the same manner as dependence on major philanthropic donors. Additionally, as previously noted, some streams of government funding such as reimbursement income for social services fail to cover costs, leaving nonprofits to find other sources to fill the gaps (Pettijohn and Boris, 2013). Similarly, nonprofits often count on established substantial streams of earned income to fund their operations and are left to scramble when those streams are cut off. Such was especially the case for arts and organizations in the pandemic. In such circumstances nonprofits often attempt to "pivot" to other forms of earned income, such as online services and sales. The case of Edwin's reflects one of many earned income strategies that nonprofit organizations have devised in crisis circumstances in order to compensate for losses of on-site customers and clients.

In general, every crisis is different and each one affects different nonprofits in different ways. "Perfect storms" are possible wherein all sources of income are seriously impacted at once. In that case, income strategies must necessarily play second fiddle to other strategies, such as reserve funds, cost-reduction options and external safety nets. But perfect storms are rare, and strategies that allow nonprofits to gain flexibility in their income structure are generally a wise investment.

INCOME DIVERSIFICATION

As already noted, diversification of income comes naturally to nonprofits, given the variety of services they offer, and the natural connections between those services and particular sources of income. (We will generally use the term "income" rather than "revenue" to account for non-monetary resources – for example, in-kind gifts and volunteering – in addition to monetary sources of support.) Indeed, research indicates not only that reliance on different sources of income (earned income, contributions, government support, and so on) varies by mission or field of service, but so does the degree of diversification in nonprofits' revenue portfolios. As reported by Chang, Tuckman and Chikoto-Schultz (2018), for example, nonprofits that rely mostly on donations are likely to be more diversified than those more reliant on earned income. Still, all nonprofits can pursue diversification from their foundational portfolios. Indeed, they tend to do so over time, as they grow larger and more administratively capable of managing different kinds of income.

In terms of resilience, research generally confirms that diversification is associated with greater financial stability, although there are caveats. Managing additional sources of income entails extra administrative costs, and in some instances nonprofit organizations may find themselves better off cultivating just one or two major sources of funding; for example, dedicated government revenue streams (Gronbjerg, 1993). However, diversification strategy is based on the proposition that different sources of income are not perfectly correlated over time; that is, earned income, charitable giving, government funding and investment income do not move completely in tandem. Historical scholarship on the nonprofit sector confirms that this is the case (Gronbjerg and Salamon, 2012). Such research to date is focused on sectoral aggregates rather than analysis of changing mixes of income for individual organizations over time. It is certainly possibly that for some organizations, riding a single horse can work well. However, history suggests that whatever that horse is, it can buck. Governments enter periods of austerity when public funds become especially constricted, pandemics can close down streams of heretofore reliable earned income, and economic recessions can damper charitable contributions and undercut returns on investments; usually these events are not synchronized in time. In the COVID-19 pandemic, for example, stock markets thrived, boosting investment income, and extra government support was forthcoming, while earned income tanked.

Research also suggests that income diversification entails a trade-off with growth; that is, less diversified nonprofits may grow faster than diversified ones, but they may also experience greater financial volatility (Chang, Tuckman and Chikoto-Schultz, 2018). This finding is consistent with investment portfolio theory, which holds that investors must make trade-offs between risk and return by choosing a portfolio that either minimizes risk to achieve a stipulated return or maximizes return for a desired limit on risk.

The implications here for nonprofit resilience here are mixed. On the one hand, growth per se can be a good thing, as larger organizations are generally more resilient. In particular, they integrate more organizational slack into their operations, slack which can be pared back to absorb shocks in a crisis. On the other hand, reliance on few sources of income increases risk, and the likelihood that a loss of income in a given crisis will be more severe. Even very big trees are known to fall, and there are few (if any) nonprofits that are "too big to fail."

All this leads to the conclusion that *prudent income diversification* is an important option for nonprofit resilience. What does this look like? First, an organization must be capable of properly administering a new source of revenue. This often requires new skills and staffing expertise, possibly involving significant cost. For example, knowing how to administer ticket sales is different from soliciting donations. Second, the organization should examine its risk/benefit trade-off. How much income volatility is it willing to tolerate and what is it willing to sacrifice in long-term growth in order to reduce that volatility? These are judgment calls that nonprofit leaders should make on the basis of their experience and the information they can muster from their organization's own track record and that of other nonprofit organizations in its industry.

BOX 6.2   COOPER UNION

Cooper Union (CU) is a small university in New York City that has provided free higher education for most of its history. It offers undergraduate and master's degree programs exclusively in architecture, fine arts and engineering. It is one of the world's leading universities in these fields, attracting students from all backgrounds to a campus with a unique culture of education based on merit, without regard to ability to pay. CU was founded by industrialist Peter Cooper in 1859. In 1902, Cooper's children gave the land where the Chrysler building now sits to CU. This serves as an endowment for the school and remains the school's largest asset. In the same year, the school received a monetary gift of $600,000 from Andrew Carnegie. The Carnegie endowment allowed the school to give full-tuition scholarships to the entire student body and allowed the addition of a daytime engineering college. The stock market collapse in the financial crisis and recession of 2008–2009 resulted in significant losses in the school's endowment and investment income. In 2009, the school's managed assets lost 14% of their value, and they continued to decline *in the years following the recession. The main revenue source remained payments of approximately $9 million annually from the owner of the Chrysler Building and $18 million in tax equivalency payments from New York City, which would be lost if CU sold the land. In 2014 CU began charging tuition, provoking major student and alumni protests, resulting in a court case leading to a consent decree that requires CU to develop a sustainable free-tuition policy. Meanwhile, CU has accelerated its charitable fundraising to become an important component of its income portfolio.*

Perhaps the best income diversification strategy follows from assessing where an organization may have failed to fully exploit its own potentials. In other words, is there low-hanging fruit that can be harvested without stressing the organization too much, in order to achieve greater stability and perhaps even some growth as well? In this quest, there are two important questions to ask: (1) Are there sources of income that follow from what the organization already produces which can easily be engaged? (2) Does the organization have underutilized assets that can be exploited to generate additional income consistent with the organization's mission?

Question 1 is a straightforward application of benefits theory (Young, 2017). If, for example, an organization is benefitting an identifiable constituency from which it has not yet drawn support, then this would be a natural way to diversify. The Cooper Union case illustrates both the opportunities and the challenges. The financial crisis and some questionable management decisions (including major capital investment in a new building) threatened its ability to provide free education to promising students regardless of ability to pay (Cooper Union, 2016). Most of the cost of this program was born historically by returns on its large endowment. The diversification options for Cooper Union were at least two-fold: charge tuitions to those students able to pay and solicit contributions from alumni who previously provided little support. While the first option challenged the mission-related commitment to "free tuition," it arguably still conformed to the spirit of the mission to serve bright students regardless of their economic circumstances. The second option was easier to pursue since alumni who were proud and thankful for the education they received were up in arms about the proposed change in tuition policy.

Question 2 involves scanning an organization's assets with an eye towards income-generating potential consistent if not congruent with the organization's mission and capabilities. Indeed, exploiting underutilized assets has been a principal focus of nonprofits' historical efforts to generate additional streams of earned income (Crimmins and Keil, 1983). Examples of this come easily to mind. The grounds of a botanical garden are a beautiful place to hold private receptions or take wedding pictures. Using off hours for this purpose can generate an additional revenue stream without too much cost or stress. Alternatively, a college or university contains a rich resource of expertise in its faculty. This is not necessarily a highly underutilized resource, but there is likely some slack to be engaged for new income-generating initiatives such as community lecture programs or non-credit executive education.

In sum, prudent income diversification offers nonprofits the potential to increase their resilience by offering responses to shocks that may impact one source of income more than another, even if the particular shocks cannot be anticipated in advance. As such it remains an important tool in the nonprofit manager's resilience toolkit.

BOX 6.3   THE RIALTO CENTER FOR THE ARTS

The Rialto Center for the Arts is a performing arts center owned and operated by Georgia State University (GSU). Originally a commercial movie theater, it closed in 1989 and fell into disrepair. In the early 1990s, GSU purchased the property for the purpose of rehabilitating the Rialto to serve as a beacon for downtown revitalization, a community face for the university and a performance venue for its music department. The Rialto Center now operates as a university department, but with several different sources of revenue, including ticket sales and charitable gifts. The revenue base of the Rialto, aside from its university-funded staff positions, has four main components: rental income, ticket sales, labor and equipment reimbursements from rentals, and contributions. The Rialto was forced to close its doors on March 11, 2020, due to the pandemic. As a result, all earned income from box office, rentals and reimbursements was cut off, contributions were reduced by half, and the Rialto lost approximately 70% of its budget. The fact that the university owns its building and also funds five staff positions directly helped the Rialto through the crisis. In essence, the university serves as a fixed source of income for the Rialto, partially shielding it from the ravages of the recession. So long as the university deems the Rialto to be important to its objectives, it is in a position to ensure the theater's survival and viability.

FIXED AND SEMI-FIXED INCOME

There are some variants of nonprofit income that can be especially helpful in building organizational resilience. Crises usually impact those sources of income that are contingent on the production of goods and services, or more generally the continuity of a nonprofit's mission-focused activities. In particular, earned income depends on customer patronage, contributions depend on donor perceptions that the organization is doing something worthwhile or is carrying out grant obligations, and government funding depends on "deliverables" for which government has contracted. (Even government "grants" tend to resemble contracts.) However, other forms of income such as returns on investments (for example, endowment funds) are qualitatively distinct in this regard. Investment returns keep flowing so long as the investment remains viable. Moreover, there are some forms of earned income, such as memberships and subscriptions, that are less sensitive to shocks and interruptions than conventional fee-for-service income or day-to-day charitable giving; that is, they tend to react more slowly and less dramatically to interruptions in activity. These latter forms of "fixed" and "semi-fixed" income can be very important in buffering the impacts of a crisis. Such was the case with the Rialto Theater, which relied on a core of steady funding (in the form of funded staff positions and free rent) from its university host to see it through the pandemic.

As noted in Chapter 4, endowments can be problematic as a source of resilience because of the restrictions placed on expending their corpuses and on the use of income generated from their investments. Nonetheless, income from endowments and other investments have the distinct advantage of being disconnected from the production of mission-related services. This income depends more on the state of the economy, the wisdom with which funds have been invested and the degree to which returns are reinvested to build the corpus over time versus being paid out for operating income. As such, this "fixed" income can be a counterpart to an organization's fixed costs, as considered in Chapter 5. When an organization with large fixed costs reduces its production, variable costs decline but fixed costs remain and can threaten the financial viability of the organization. If the organization has fixed revenues to offset fixed costs, it is better positioned to survive.

To put this into perspective, investment income is generally a minor source of income for nonprofit organizations, well behind earned, contributed and government-funded income for the sector as a whole, in the United States and elsewhere. This varies by field of service, but even for the arts and education, it hovers around 10% of total revenues. Moreover, within any given field, most of the investment revenues are harvested by relatively few large institutions. As noted in Chapter 4, the decision to tie up funds into endowments is complex, and it is often sensible for smaller organizations to forego endowments in favor of more flexible ways of generating and expending income. However, the idea of fixed income can be extended to other invested resources, for purposes of building resilience. One obvious alternative is to build up non-endowment funds such as relatively liquid reserve funds, sinking funds for construction that are depleted as the projects are carried out, and strategic investment funds to seed innovations and experimental programs.

Nonprofit governing boards can also designate endowments themselves; in such cases, they have the discretion to remove restrictions without having to appeal to donors or go to court. These various kinds of funds can be liquidated more easily than traditional endowments in a crisis, but while in place they can also generate investment returns to help offset fixed costs. This offers a double value in terms of resilience: In the short term investment returns help offset fixed costs, delaying onset of a crisis. And in a full-blown crisis they can be liquidated to address emergencies.

Another income strategy is to pursue forms of income that have some "inertia" and are slow to shrink as production or activity diminishes. We can call these "semi-fixed" sources of revenue because they do not quickly disappear when activity is interrupted. Moreover, they can sometimes serve a dual purpose if those who supply these funds want to be charitable to the organization in a crisis situation. Memberships, subscriptions and gift cards are some examples. Thus, some members of a YMCA or Jewish Community Center who care about these institutions and want some assurance that they will return to full capacity after the crisis are willing to continue to pay their membership fees even if their access to services and facilities is reduced or even suspended in a crisis. Similarly season ticket holders for nonprofit orchestras and theaters may be willing to hold onto their tickets rather than ask for refunds, even if a season is canceled, in the expectation that they will be exchanged for post-crisis performances.

Indeed, the charitable impulse for members and subscribers can extend further than just a willingness to hold on and be patient, but actually to engage these mechanisms as a way of providing explicit charitable support, particularly in a crisis situation. Some nonprofits, such as museums, botanical gardens and churches, view membership revenues essentially as charitable contributions as much as they consider them to be fees for services and benefits. For other nonprofits, such as theaters, orchestras and community centers, that package their sales into subscriptions and memberships, crises offer opportunities to appeal to their loyal customers to purchase future performances with this charitable notion in mind, thus slowing the erosion of this revenue source in a crisis. To go even further, the purchase of gift cards for future consumption either for themselves or others is another way that loyal customers can show their support in a crisis. Gift cards may not always be cashed in, providing a bonus to the nonprofit, but even if they are eventually used, they will have served the purpose of helping the organization weather the situation when it was most severe.

The concept of fixed income applies to charitable giving as well. Contributors can be asked to become "sustainers" committed to regular contributions over time, a strategy used by some public radio stations in the United States. And major donors reluctant to commit to providing endowments over which they lose control may be more comfortable with so-called "evergreen grants" that promise continuity of a grant into the indefinite future. The Mandel Foundations in Cleveland used this device for many years to fund university programs. Short of this, major donors can also be urged to provide multi-year unrestricted and renewable grants so that recipient nonprofits can plan for their future stability and resilience.

The focus on "loyal customers" is an important feature of semi-fixed revenue. As Hirschman (1970) argued, loyalty is an important source of organizational slack that can make the difference between failure and survival in a situation that threatens an organization's income. In Hirschman's terms, loyalty underwrites a more "inelastic demand" that provides a brake on revenue losses in a crisis.

SUMMARY

The keys to income resilience strategies for nonprofits in crisis are *redundancy* and *decoupling*. Within the framework of benefits theory, nonprofits can make their basic decisions about the composition of their income portfolios to reflect their logical sources of support. This provides the foundation for diversified income portfolios customized to each organization's particular mission and services. In terms of resilience, the resulting redundancy of income sources also serves as a shock absorber to help management through crises. That redundancy can be achieved by fully exploiting all potential income sources consistent with mission. Having distinctly different sources of income that do not respond identically to crises, and which have some potential for filling in for one another, is an important way to build an income resilience strategy. There are at least three levels at which this income resiliency can be developed. The first is to balance distinctly different sources of income – principally earned income, gifts and grants, government funding, gifts-in-kind and investment income – guided by benefits theory. This is likely to be the most impactful option, given that these sources tend not to vary in perfect tandem over time. A second level is to diversify sources within such categories; for example, to have contracts with multiple government agencies, or grants from multiple foundations. This can be helpful, although multiple sources are likely to be subject to the same stresses and to react in similar ways in a crisis. Thus, within-source diversification may be somewhat limited in its resilience value. A third level is to develop new sources of income, especially if nonprofits can identify underutilized assets with income-generating potential, or natural sources they have not yet fully exploited (such as tuitions and alumni gifts in the case of Cooper Union). The latter can be an important strategy in preparation and buffering against crises but is difficult to initiate in crisis mode itself when attentions are diverted, and all hands are already on deck to douse the fire.

Second, nonprofit organizations can build their income resilience by cultivating sources that are *decoupled* from the impacts of a crisis. This is most easily considered in terms of fixed and semi-fixed sources of income that are relatively insensitive to reductions and closures of the organization's normal activities and production of services. Investment income is a major focus of decoupling strategy, through endowments and other invested funds. So is developing membership and subscription strategies that leverage the patience and charitable impulses of loyal customers and supporters, or coaxing donors to be "sustainers" committed to continuing contributions over time.

REFERENCES

Candid (2021). *Philanthropy and COVID-19*. New York, NY: Candid and the Center for Disaster Philanthropy.

Chang, Cyril F., Howard P. Tuckman and Grace L. Chikoto-Schultz (2018). "Income Diversity and Nonprofit Financial Health," chapter 1 in Bruce A. Seaman and Dennis R. Young (eds), *Handbook of Research on Nonprofit Economics and Management*. Cheltenham, UK and Northampton, MA: Edward Elgar Publishing, pp.11–34.

Cooper Union (2016). "About Cooper Union." www.cooper.edu/about.

Crimmins, James C., and Mary Keil (1983). *Enterprise in the Nonprofit Sector*. Washington, DC: Partners for Livable Places and the Rockefeller Brothers Fund.

Gronbjerg, Kirsten A. (1993). *Understanding Nonprofit Funding*. San Francisco, CA: Jossey-Bass.

Gronbjerg, Kirsten A., and Lester Salamon (2012). "Devolution, Marketization and the Changing Shape of Nonprofit–Government Relations," chapter 15 in Lester M. Salamon (ed.), *The State of Nonprofit America*. Washington, DC: Brookings Institution Press, pp.549–586.

Hirschman, Albert O. (1970). *Exit, Voice and Loyalty*. Cambridge, MA: Harvard University Press.

National Council of Nonprofits (2022). "The American Rescue Plan Act." www.councilofnonprofits.org/trends-policy-issues/the-american-rescue-plan-act.

Pettijohn, Sarah L., and Elizabeth T. Boris (2013). *Contracts and Grants between Nonprofits and Government*. Brief #3, December. Washington, DC: Urban Institute.

"Rialto Center for the Arts: Persevering during Covid," *Emerities* newsletter for emeritus faculty of Georgia State University, summer 2020.

Wikipedia (2022). "The Salvation Army Ray & Joan Kroc Corps Community Centers." https://en.wikipedia.org/wiki/The_Salvation_Army_Ray_%26_Joan_Kroc_Corps_Community_Centers.

Young, Dennis R. (2017). *Financing Nonprofits and Other Social Enterprises*. Cheltenham, UK and Northampton, MA: Edward Elgar Publishing.

Cartoon 7   When the internet went down, I knew my abacus would come in handy!

7. Technology and resilience

One definition of technology is "the practical application of knowledge" (*Webster's Desk Dictionary*, 1983). Over the course of history, technology has radically changed the way in which humans sustain themselves and live their lives, from the agricultural revolution to the industrial revolution, to today's digital age. In modern parlance, the term "technology" is commonly associated with the use of advanced computerized systems of communication, data management and control, in transportation, the military, medicine, consumer products and many other fields. In the public's mind, such technology is not a particularly outstanding feature of nonprofit organizations; after all, nonprofits are service-oriented and generally labor-intensive – not generally prone to automation and robotic solutions. However, the importance of technology in the nonprofit sector is undercounted in various respects. First, some fields where nonprofits are prominent, such as health care, are critically dependent on high tech. Second, nonprofits are integrated into the broader economy which has adopted modern communications and computer technology into day-to-day business across the board. In recent years, nonprofits have had to overhaul their operations, just to keep up with the times. Currently, nonprofits are active in social media and use computers for business purposes like organizations in any other sector. Third, and most importantly, the concept of technology is generic, not just the modern version of digitization and automation. As we will discuss, technology is simply the way in which the work of an organization gets done. The COVID-19 pandemic clearly demonstrated that nonprofits have found new ways to be resilient by adjusting the technologies through which they carry out their mission-related work.

WHAT IS ORGANIZATIONAL TECHNOLOGY?

Economists characterize technology with a construction called a "production function" (Young, Steinberg, Emanuele and Simmons, 2019) which is simply a mathematical way of specifying how inputs such as labor, equipment and supplies are transformed into outputs such as clients served, performances produced or donated dollars raised. In many instances, nonprofits have choices among the technologies they can use. A development department can use mass mailings, e-mail solicitations, personal communications or some combination thereof to raise money. An organization designed to feed the hungry can run a soup kitchen or deliver meals on wheels. In the COVID-19 pandemic, many nonprofits had to choose between in-person, on-site delivery of performances, exhibitions, lessons or counseling sessions, and on-line substitutes. Many organizations demonstrated their resilience by "pivoting" to new modes of delivery – that is, to alternative technologies – when they were inhibited by circumstances from carrying out their work in conventional ways. Some organizations were better prepared to do this than others. Not surprisingly, for example, those nonprofits that were more computer-savvy before the crisis were more successful in weathering the crisis (Salesforce.org, 2021).

In order to properly understand resilience and technology in the nonprofit sector, we need to take a broad view of economists' notion of the production function. In particular, most nonprofits must be concerned with the impacts of their decisions beyond the particular outputs that they produce. Thus, schools want to know how their students progressed in their knowledge, not just how many lessons they delivered in a given period of time. That is, they are concerned with "outcomes" more than "outputs." This is important because there can be many different ways of producing outcomes; moreover, outcomes are usually a product of both what the organization does and other environmental factors influencing its clients. Thus, consideration of alternative technologies offers the opportunity for real innovation by discovering wholly different ways to accomplish mission-related goals. For example, schools are discovering new benefits of on-line learning that they will seek to preserve even in a non-crisis situation.

BOX 7.2   THE AKRON SYMPHONY ORCHESTRA

During the COVID-19 pandemic, the Akron Symphony Orchestra in Akron, Ohio suspended its regular concert series and developed its Interlude program which broke up the orchestra into smaller ensembles that could appear in safe and accessible community venues. Not only did this minimize transmission risk among orchestra members, but it also provided a safer environment to concertgoers. It also allowed the orchestra to perform in venues for audiences that had not been reached before. The orchestra also offered new on-line educational content and free programming to help promote subscriptions to the 2021–2022 season.

TECHNOLOGY STRATEGIES AND RESILIENCE

During the COVID-19 pandemic, nonprofits experimented with a number of different kinds of technology resilience strategies. The most common approach was to substitute or complement their on-site services with on-line versions. This allowed them to accommodate necessary restrictions on on-site work by their employees, and on-site consumption of their services by clients and consumers. Examples of this abound. Schools went to remote learning, museums put their exhibitions on-line, musical ensembles and theaters stitched together on-line performances, medical personnel provided telemedicine consultations, and scholars at universities and think tanks collaborated on research projects through virtual networks.

In many instances, of course, physical operation is intrinsically required or at least highly desirable. But even here, new technological options were employed. Food was brought to the needy via new local delivery services to overcome the fact that clients were homebound or quarantined. Some nonprofits like Deep Vellum and public libraries developed curbside delivery or found ways to distribute literary content on-line. And new ways were found to care for children and assist them with on-line learning (in community centers, for example) so that parents deemed to be essential workers could go to work. Moreover, nonprofits found new ways to provide on-site services that could conform with pandemic restrictions. For example, musical ensembles such as the Akron Symphony performed in small groups and in smaller venues, rather than having full orchestras play to large, crowded concert halls. Schools moved classes to outdoor settings. Community centers implemented computer reservation systems to regulate the use of exercise equipment and swimming lanes.

What do these experiences say about the nature of nonprofit technology resilience strategies? These strategies work when they exhibit one or more of the following characteristics: complementarity, redundancy and innovation.

Complementarity means that the new ways of operating can work effectively alongside the traditional methods. This characteristic allows the organization to run both modes at once, as needed, to expand the alternative mode when the traditional mode is constricted and to reverse the process when the crisis subsides. In the pandemic, for example, schools ran on-line and on-site learning in complementary ways, expanding on-line learning when on-site operation had to be closed and cutting it back when schools could open again. In the transition, both modes could run simultaneously, and after the crisis an effective (perhaps new) combination of the two could be carried on.

Redundancy means that a new technology can substitute for the original one and that parallel technologies can be held in reserve so that responses can be mounted to various kinds of crisis. For example, in the pandemic, having on-line capability was a great advantage to many nonprofits, positioning them to expand when on-site delivery was shut down. But the opposite could also occur. A natural disaster such as a lightning storm, or a man-made catastrophe such as a cyberattack, could shut down on-line operations for a long period of time. Having backup with traditional technologies such as on-site instruction or counseling services would enable organizations to navigate through the crisis until digital capacity was restored.

Innovation means that a new technology enables the organization to achieve better results than it could under traditional methods. This is the essence of the old adage that necessity is the mother of invention. In the pandemic, nonprofits found lots of new ways of doing things, and some of these ways will be retained after the crisis because they were simply better or more effective. Universities learned, for example, that they could expand their markets by putting coursework on-line because students would no longer be required to be within commuting distance. Many nonprofits found that they could allow some of their employees to work at home effectively, permitting savings in the costs of office space and parking lots. Nonprofit arts agencies found that they could appeal to new groups that would not ordinarily visit a museum or attend a concert, by putting their offerings on-line. It is doubtful that these organizations will return fully to their old ways after the crisis is over.

Innovation can play a double role in building organizational resilience through technology. First, innovation alters the production function. If one thinks about all the possible ways in which an organization's inputs (staff, physical plant and equipment, supplies, and so on) can be combined and deployed using a given technology in order to achieve its mission-related goals, then adding a new technology can only expand the possibilities. Some of the resulting combinations may actually produce better results than before. For example, some combinations of on-line and on-site learning may yield better results in student achievement than on-site programming alone. Similarly, adding a telemedicine option to the repertoire of a mental health organization can improve client access as well as service quality and capacity by employing professionals and engaging clients beyond its local geographical region. In such ways, new technology essentially creates new capacity to respond to a crisis, or in the long run to achieve greater ongoing performance capacity.

Second, innovation is a way of thinking for long-term resilience. In essence, organizations that embody a culture of innovation are more likely to be resilient in a crisis because they are focused on problem-solving. This is where the economist's concept of a production function again comes into play, appropriately construed to focus on outcomes rather than outputs. In an organization with a culture of innovation, managers and staff continually ask how, with the resources at hand, they can achieve better results. This can lead to one of two possible kinds of benefits: more effective use of the technology at hand or development of technological improvements or indeed whole new technologies. In these ways, the organization becomes more resilient because it can rely on its culture to generate solutions in a crisis. Technological innovation is an important aspect of organizational learning, as discussed in chapters 3 and 11, a basic feature of resilient organizations.

According to a study by Salesforce (2021), nonprofit organizations have used digital technology to manage the COVID-19 pandemic and build resilience along a variety of dimensions, including navigating shifts in their operations, revising their services to serve different clients or new audiences, moving programs on-line, developing new methods to reach new recipients of their current services and adding new services to attract new audiences. The Salesforce survey finds that nonprofits with "high digital maturity" are more effective in carrying out these initiatives than those with "low digital maturity." Moreover, the report hints at how technology is integrally tied to the broad spectrum of organizational resilience strategies discussed throughout this book. An interesting issue here is whether a nonprofit's digital sophistication aligns with that of its clientele. It does little good if fancy new services are offered on-line if clients are not computer-savvy. Thus, engagement with stakeholders is an important component of technological innovation in the nonprofit sector.

TECHNOLOGY AND OTHER RESILIENCE STRATEGIES

Technology-based strategies are just one way to build nonprofit organizational resilience. However, technology is also central to other dimensions of resilience-building. In this book we consider alternative strategies based on restructuring costs, expanding sources of income, exploiting assets, strategically managing human resources, developing collaborative relationships and pursuing entrepreneurial initiatives designed to bolster resilience. Each of these approaches can have important technological components.

Technology can assist in developing cost-related resilience. For example, nonprofits can take advantage of economies of scale by outsourcing back-office functions such as accounting, ticketing and even fundraising to larger, specialized organizations with advanced systems. Such options also eliminate fixed costs since they can be engaged on an as-needed basis, rather than maintaining a permanent infrastructure. As explained in Chapter 5, these strategies can fundamentally enhance an organization's resilience over time.

Technology can also contribute to income-based resilience strategies. Indeed, new technologies such as crowdsourcing or search algorithms to identify possible new donors, and programs to track and maintain donor and consumer loyalty, can be used to diversify an organization's income portfolio, a basic resilience strategy as discussed in Chapter 6. New technology can also be helpful in building memberships and subscriptions, forms of income that may be less volatile in a crisis than ordinary fee or contributions income.

Indeed, technological innovations can underwrite strategies to make better use of an organization's assets, leading to important shifts in the way a nonprofit organization carries out its work (that is, its own core technology). For example, a nonprofit garden club run by volunteers might recognize the value of its assets for generating commercial income through facilities rentals, consultations based on its expertise and sales of garden products using its brand value. These assets could be marketed through modern means of communications such as social media and the internet. In the process, the organization could be transformed into a more robust and resilient botanical garden capable of supporting itself through multiple sources of income. This is essentially the story of the Garden Club of Cleveland, which transformed itself over a period of years into the Cleveland Botanical Garden. (Of course, such a transformation can generate other vulnerabilities which would require further scrutiny.)

Building resilience through networking and collaboration, as examined in Chapter 10, is another area where technology can play an important role. Collaborative networks are built and maintained through communications, and effective communications require robust communications networks. For example, nonprofit federations use their communications networks to monitor, assist, educate and advise their members in good times and bad. Building relationships between headquarters and affiliates and among affiliates themselves (a kind of social capital) creates a pool of trust that can be tapped for help and for coordinated response in a crisis situation. While old-fashioned telephone calls, face-to-face visits and e-mail correspondence all have their place in cultivating and strengthening networks, modern digital technology has expanded the potential for network resilience-building.

Additionally, technology can be an important component of nonprofit human resource resilience strategy, as discussed in Chapter 8. Indeed, the COVID-19 pandemic amply demonstrated that nonprofits were able to maintain much of their operations by developing their capacities for staff and volunteers to work on-line. Modern technology permitted this short-term resilience and it also is likely to lead to more effective and flexible operations in the future by identifying better balances of on-site and on-line working over the longer term. In general, crises demand flexibility in deploying an organization's workforce, leading to greater complexity in workforce management. Technology can be an important part of managing that complexity more effectively.

Finally, technology can be an important component of an entre-preneurship-based resilience strategy, as considered in Chapter 9. In the business sector, a significant proportion of entrepreneurial activity is on-line. New businesses take the form of apps that can capture the attention of venture capitalists and demonstrate new sources of demand. Moreover, established tech companies continually upgrade and modify their programs to attract customers and advertisers, or they buy out new successful startup ventures. The nonprofit sector is not so aggressive or vicious in its technological compe-tition, but technology remains a frontier for nonprofits to build their capacity for services and resources, not only for current success but for long-term resil-ience. In the COVID-19 pandemic, for example, museums have found whole new audiences by putting their collections on-line, and community centers have enhanced their portfolio of services by providing parents with assistance to help children learn on-line.

BOX 7.3   THE ROYAL NATIONAL THEATRE

Although the Royal National Theatre (RNT) has an international reputa-tion, the focus of its programming has been delivering plays and musicals live in theaters in the United Kingdom. When these venues were closed during the COVID-19 pandemic, RNT capitalized on historical record-ings of plays with famous actors (such as James Corden and Benedict Cumberbatch) by making them available for free viewing on-line. These sixteen plays were viewed a combined total of fifteen million times in 173 countries. This established the foundation for a subscription streaming service that will provide a new, international revenue stream even after COVID (National Theatre, 2022).

INNOVATION, LEADERSHIP AND ORGANIZATIONAL CULTURE

Technological resilience requires nonprofit organizations to innovate. But what do we know about how to make organizations more innovative? We noted above that a "culture of innovation" enhances an organization's resilience by emphasizing a problem-solving mindset. However, research on organizational culture in nonprofit organizations does not unequivocally associate a "strong" culture with innovation. If, as summarized by Kristina Jaskyte (2011), a strong culture means that the organization's members hold homogeneously to the same values and principles, then organizational scholars disagree: some hold that a strong culture underpins innovation, while others argue that strong cultures actually undermine innovation by discouraging organizational members from challenging existing ways of doing things. Indeed, Jaskyte's (2011) own empirical research on nonprofit organizations does not find cultural consensus to be a significant determinant of innovation, one way or another. However, that research does find that "transformational leadership" which "encourages followers to be creative and think of new ideas" (p.80) is positively and significantly related to both technological and administrative innovation in the nonprofit organizations that Jaskyte studied.

This debate among researchers offers an optimistic message for nonprofit leaders: nonprofits are capable of cultivating resilience through technology. The question becomes who champions it (ideally a transformational leader) and what resilience-related purpose is served by the technology: complementarity, redundancy and/or innovation. The purposes can even be sequential; as seen in the RNT case, providing sixteen free plays with famous actors (an *innovation* in helping people appreciate the arts) has also yielded a *complementarity* through a subscription streaming service as stage performances begin again. This should not be surprising, but it does underline the importance of the entrepreneurial mindset in building organizational resilience by encouraging nonprofit organizations to think broadly about new ways of doing things, both within the context of a crisis and for remaining resilient once the crisis passes.

SUMMARY

Generically, technology is the manner in which an organization transforms input resources (labor, equipment, facilities, supplies) into outputs (for example, clients served) and outcomes (for example, health improved). While in recent times technology has been largely associated with computers and digital communications, technology-related resilience strategy should be thought of more broadly as the alternative means and methods through which a nonprofit organization can achieve its mission. Successful technology-based resilience strategies work because they offer nonprofit organizations some combination of complementarity, redundancy and innovation regarding their current ways of addressing their missions and achieving their outcomes. Moreover, technology-based strategies are often integrally involved with other aspects of resilience strategy as discussed in other chapters, including adaptation of cost structures, diversification of income sources, building of network relationships, deploying human resources, entrepreneurial problem-solving, and monitoring and measuring performance and risk. In recent crises such as the COVID-19 pandemic, nonprofits have been enormously resourceful in employing new technologies to deliver their services online or to re-orient their services to accommodate crisis-related constraints on consumer and staff mobility. They have also employed technology to expand their markets, providing new opportunities to both adjust their operations in the current crisis and to build their resilience for future challenges.

REFERENCES

Jaskyte, Kristina (2011). "Predictors of Administrative and Technological Innovations in Nonprofit Organizations." *Public Administration Review*, January/February, 77–86.

National Theatre (2022). "Facts and Figures for 2020/21." www.nationaltheatre.org.uk/about-the-national-theatre/key-facts-and-figures.

Salesforce.org (2021). *Nonprofit Trends Report*, 3rd Edition. www.salesforce.org/wp-content/uploads/2021/01/ngo-trends-report-third-edition-122120-v2.pdf.

Webster's Desk Dictionary of the English Language (1983). "Technology." New York, NY: Portland House, p.919.

Young, Dennis R., Richard Steinberg, Rosemarie Emanuele and Walter O. Simmons (2019). *Economics for Nonprofit Managers and Social Entrepreneurs*. Cheltenham, UK and Northampton, MA: Edward Elgar Publishing.

Cartoon 8   *When they said RIFs I didn't know they were talking about my job!*

8.   People and resilience

*The Girl Scout Council of Northeast Ohio (GSNEO) covers an
eighteen-county region and serves some 17,200 girls, and 9,000 adult
members of whom approximately 2,500 are volunteers and the rest supporters of GSNEO. Membership declined substantially in 2020–2021
from its pre-pandemic level of 23,500 and has since been rebuilding.
Loss of revenues from memberships and programming required GSNEO
to make adjustments to its paid workforce, including a reduction in its
full-time staff of 86 people. A combination of strategies, including buyout
offers and salary reductions for higher-paid staff, were used to reduce
payroll. Twelve staff took buyouts and only two layoffs were required.
These changes allowed the Council to maintain operations while minimizing disruption of the workforce. Initially most of the staff were able to
work from home, and later transitioned to a combination of remote and
in-office work. Troop meetings and programming for girls moved on-line,
and summer camp in 2020 was held virtually. In general, volunteers were
not used to supplement the paid workforce. Indeed, GSNEO is careful to
differentiate volunteer and staff responsibilities so that volunteers do not
perform staff duties and staff members may not hold volunteer positions.*

Nonprofit organizations are "labor-intensive" – they are highly reliant on
people to carry out their work, much more so than most businesses. This is
because they produce services that are not easily automated and because their
interactions with, and impacts on, clients, consumers and communities require
personal communications and relationships. Some nonprofits are more reliant
on capital assets than others – for example, hospitals, universities and art
centers require substantial physical plants – but all are critically dependent on
the dedication and productivity of their workforces. For this reason, a nonprofit
organization cannot be resilient unless its workforce is managed for resilience,
no matter what other strategies are employed.

At the same time, managing human resources (HR) for resilience is extraordinarily complex. The COVID-19 pandemic revealed the manifold workforce decisions that nonprofits were required to make. If they were faced with reducing costs, as many organizations such as GSNEO were when they had to shut down or curtail their operations, they needed to figure out how to consolidate their workforces – by considering a variety of options, including layoffs, furloughs, reduction of hours, consolidation of positions, reductions in compensation and substitutions of volunteer for paid labor. If they were faced with demands to expand rapidly to address the crisis, as were some organizations such as foodbanks and hospitals, they again needed to figure out how to do so by considering multiple options, such as recruiting volunteers, hiring new staff on a short-term contractual or salaried basis, or engaging existing staff for overtime work. Add to this the fact that many nonprofit workers faced new personal stresses stemming from the crisis, including fears about their own health and that of their families and new levels of responsibility caring for children who were homebound or relatives who were ill. Indeed, the latter fed into yet another level of nonprofit HR decision making – the degree to which employees could be deployed to work at home versus coming to the office or going to sites where they could service their clients in person. Finally, as nonprofits experienced in the COVID-19 pandemic, labor market conditions can change unpredictably. In particular, a contraction of the labor force in the United States put upward pressure on wages, making it more difficult for some nonprofits, especially in the social services, to pay competitive wages in order to retain or recruit workers (Casselman, 2021). This led to worker shortages and elevated job vacancy rates (National Council of Nonprofits, 2021), which affected the ability of nonprofits to both cope in the short term and rebuild their workforces for long-term resilience.

Resilience requires nonprofit managers and leaders to consider their manifold HR decisions in a manner that will see their organizations through a crisis at hand and strengthen the organization to navigate future crises more successfully. As we discuss below, there are no simple formulas, but there are systematic ways to think through these decisions that should be integrated into an overall regime of nonprofit resilience management.

COLLECTIVE WISDOM ABOUT HUMAN RESOURCES MANAGEMENT FROM RESEARCH AND PRACTICE

There is substantial literature about managing people in organizations, focusing mostly on the business sector but with important recent contributions to understanding nonprofit workforces as well. Little of this literature is concerned specifically with managing for resilience or navigating and preparing for crises. However, important and relevant insights can be gleaned from the general findings and principles identified in this body of knowledge, and these ideas can be applied to nonprofit resilience management.

A good place to start is with Lucassen's (2021) comprehensive and wide-ranging history of work over the course of human experience. Lucassen argues that work is necessary not only for survival but that "the sense of fulfillment it brings makes it indispensable for our self-esteem and the regard of our peers" (p.12). He notes that in modern times (the last three centuries), theorists ranging from Adam Smith to Karl Marx have viewed labor as central to producing value in society while at the same time modernization has posed important risks to workers. In particular, he is concerned with stagnation in pay over the past several decades due to declines in unionization and other factors, as well as losses of workers' security stemming from globalization and growth of organizational practices such as outsourcing and independent contracting (the gig economy). Looking forward, Lucassen argues that work offers a sense of meaning that leisure cannot provide and a source of social connection that people require, but also that people need to feel they are fairly treated both within organizations and in society at large, noting the growing inequality of income in the United States and elsewhere in recent years. The last sentences in his book capture lessons for the future:

> In this phase of history, the idea is growing that we have new opportunities to decide ... what our working lives will look like. Our long past as humankind suggests strongly that when making such choices, we must not lose sight of three principles – meaning, cooperation and fairness – that can be derived from this story of work. (p.437)

The overall lesson we can derive from this history of work is that it is important to pay attention to workers' aspirations and values as difficult decisions are made about workforce adjustments and the building of a productive and resilient labor force for the future. We argue here that this is both a long- and short-term issue: A satisfied and productive workforce is better able to weather crisis situations.

In the business sector, Ulrich and his colleagues (2012) investigated the competencies required for HR professionals going forward. Many of their recommendations also imply the need for building long-term resilience. In their view, "Sustainability requires a long-term view, an integrated solution, and an ability to learn and innovate" (p.23). Moreover, an HR professional should "be an HR change champion who connects the past with the future and who anticipates and manages individual initiative and institutional change" (p.23). The Ulrich team suggests that organizational assessments of HR move from a narrow efficiency perspective to a *capability* orientation that includes collaboration, innovation and ability to manage risk (p.117). Ultimately these scholars envision "abundant organizations" that seek resilience by persevering "to develop people and products," "encouraging learning from both successes and setbacks" and recovering "when things go wrong" (p.128). To Ulrich and his colleagues, change is a necessary part of the world, so the key is embracing it in the right way in order to harness innovation – and people are the key.

Ton (2014) sees the HR function as central to the success of businesses. Her analysis posits virtuous or vicious cycles of organizational performance based on investment or disinvestment in the workforce. In her model, good HR practices and investment in the workforce lead to a better quality of labor. This in turn leads to better operational performance which results in greater financial and organizational success, while the reverse process is true for disinvestment and poor HR practices. Investing in the labor force requires better pay and benefits, and greater opportunities for individual growth and achievement. Her "good jobs" strategies include cross-training so that employees are able to support and fill in for one another, and building slack into the workforce. She sees slack as valuable not only for responding to peaks in demand but also for capacity to pursue continuous improvements in slower periods. Similarly, cross-training not only provides the organization with flexibility to get work done in a dynamic environment, but it also raises morale by offering employees a greater sense of teamwork and of their value to the organization as a whole. Ton argues that these strategies allow the organization to more easily adapt to change and to manage for the long term.

Several recent review articles focus specifically on HR practices in the nonprofit sector. Watson and Abzug (2016) document that workers in the nonprofit sector tend to be more intrinsically motivated than workers in other sectors. As a result, they are more deeply engaged in their value-driven organizations, more productive but also subject to overextending themselves. This dedication and embeddedness offers loyalty to the organization and an edge in retention of staff, but also puts workers at risk of burnout or temptations to leave for more lucrative opportunities; it also makes them more difficult to replace. Thus, practices such as layoffs and outsourcing require considerable caution and mindfulness, because of the potential losses of valuable, sometimes unique, human capital. In all, Watson and Abzug emphasize that long-term success of a nonprofit organization requires building an effective HR culture that reflects all of these concerns.

Leete (2006) explores the evidence on wage differences between nonprofits and organizations in other sectors. While it is commonly believed that wages are lower in the nonprofit sector, Leete finds that this is not uniformly the case. Indeed, circumstances (labor markets) differ from industry to industry within the sector and overall there is no significant difference, although it is clear that executives in the nonprofit sector tend to be paid less than their peers elsewhere.

BOX 8.2 ANGEL FLIGHT SOUTH CENTRAL

Volunteer pilots are the core of the services offered by Angel Flight South Central (AFSC), which provides air travel for patients in need of medical care. Pilots cannot be compensated for either their time or fuel, so AFSC needs to be creative in showing its appreciation. Discount programs with partner organizations, jackets and practical items that can be used during missions, like branded blankets – all are ways that AFSC has found to acknowledge the commitment of its pilot team.

THE ROLE OF VOLUNTEERS

A special feature of the nonprofit workforce is its very substantial engagement of volunteers, as exemplified by AFSC, GSNEO and numerous other nonprofit organizations. Leete (2006) estimates that there are six volunteers for every paid worker in the U.S. nonprofit sector, although this does not normalize for hours worked. Still, there is no question that volunteers constitute a very substantial portion of the nonprofit workforce and an extremely important source of the sector's resilience.

Leete also examines the variety of motivations for volunteering. She distinguishes between voluntary and obligatory giving of one's time, the latter reflecting moral obligations, and between intrinsic and extrinsic motivations, the former reflecting satisfaction from the act of volunteering itself. In contrast, extrinsic motivations reflect *results* gained from volunteering, including instrumental (satisfaction from outcomes), psychological (based on altruistic and egoistic values of the volunteer), human capital (building of job skills and marketability) and social capital (building of social networks) benefits. Leete's distinctions are echoed by Eliasoph (2020), especially the degree to which volunteer motivations may be driven in part by moral obligation as well as coercive factors in certain institutional contexts. Regardless of these distinctions, the multiplicity and complexity of volunteer motivations speaks to the challenges of volunteer management and the nuances of building a volunteer workforce that underpins organizational resilience.

Interestingly, Leete also reviews the relationship between volunteering and charitable giving where she finds these activities to be economic complements, in the sense that people do not see volunteering and contributing money as alternative choices or trade-offs but rather as activities that go hand in hand and build on one another. This has important implications for resilience, as engagement of volunteers can help address both HR and financial needs in crisis situations and over the long term.

Brudney (2016) offers a comprehensive review of research-based knowledge about volunteer management. He confirms that volunteers are not free and that their engagement comes with costs. In contemplating volunteer engagement to supplement or substitute for paid staff, Brudney argues for a criterion of cost/effectiveness comparing relative mission impacts per dollar for each in particular circumstances. He also observes that substituting volunteers for paid staff may cause resentment among paid staff; hence paid staff should be involved in volunteer recruitment and deployment if only because there can be substantial overlap of staff and volunteer responsibilities that must be sorted out and coordinated. Still, volunteers can be seen as an important source of help in times of fiscal stress and crisis and may be especially adept in fundraising. Other tasks for which volunteers are found to be especially suited include those which may be performed periodically or episodically rather than on a regular schedule; those that do not require specialized training or expertise; those that may require a specialized skill not found on staff; and those that can be carried out off-site, for example on-line. Brudney also confirms that volunteers are largely motivated by desires to help people and to do something useful, and that their retention depends on the friendships and internal relationships they develop during their time in the organization. Finally, he notes that the rate of volunteering in a given year in the United States has remained fairly stable over time, at roughly a quarter of the adult population, suggesting that volunteers are not an inexhaustible resource upon which nonprofits can draw in building their resilience.

While the literature does not specifically focus on HR strategies for building organizational resilience and navigating crises, it contains valuable lessons that can be applied to these challenges. Certainly, we have learned that managing the workforce well is central to organizational success over time, and hence resilience. Towards this end, workers need to find meaning in their work as well as adequate compensation. They need also to enjoy social connections in their organizations and feel they are treated fairly. These requirements seem to be especially applicable to nonprofits as values-based, social mission-oriented organizations. The literature also suggests that wise HR management should focus on the long term, engaging a workforce that can learn from experience and be innovative and creative in solving problems and improving performance. Building capacity (or capabilities) rather than making decisions simply on the basis of short-term efficiency is required, and redundancy is suggested through adequate margins of slack and cross-training of personnel. Finally, reliance on volunteers is a source of considerable value and potential resilience for nonprofit organizations, but determining appropriate levels of paid versus volunteer staff requires accounting for important nuances, including: differences in cost/effectiveness of volunteers and paid staff for various organizational tasks, interdependencies and possible tensions between paid staff and volunteers, correlations between volunteering and charitable giving, limits to the supply of volunteers and the wide variety of volunteer motivations.

CRITERIA FOR HUMAN RESOURCES RESILIENCE

Given these lessons from the literature, we argue here that managing nonprofit HR resources for resilience requires *flexibility, fairness and foresight.*

First, organizations must have flexibility to adjust their workforces to meet the demands of a crisis. As noted, this is likely to entail workforce and/or payroll reductions, or sometimes augmentations. For example, as discussed in Chapter 4, permanent salaried staff represent a fixed cost that may not be sustainable under conditions of revenue loss. Strategies that permit a reallocation from permanent paid staff to volunteers and part-time contract workers essentially convert fixed to variable costs, providing the flexibility that may be required to navigate a crisis. Similarly, a policy that facilitates expansion through volunteer recruitment and part-time hiring underwrites the flexibility to expand to meet new demands in a crisis. However, HR research counsels that these are not simple economic decisions, because they can have serious impacts on organizational culture, human and social capital embedded in staff, and the internal balance of the workforce going forward. Indeed, poor HR decisions risk triggering a vicious cycle of disinvestment as described by Ton (2014).

Second, resilience requires fairness. The literature makes it clear that HR decisions which are perceived as "unfair" by an organization's workers can undermine an organization's morale and the motivation of its workers to perform well under the stress of crisis or to maintain the dedication and enthusiasm for building a stronger organization in the longer term. Fairness can be judged along multiple lines and may vary from one context to another. Workers with seniority may feel that they deserve preferential treatment because of their records of service to the organization, or perhaps promises made to them over the years. Workers from certain groups defined by race, ethnicity, age, gender or sexual orientation may feel that they deserve special consideration because of historical discrimination, compatibility with the organization's current clientele, lack of past opportunities or the fact that the crisis is having an especially severe impact on them. (The latter applied particularly to women and essential workers in the pandemic who had to care for children whose schools pivoted to on-line instruction.) And low-paid workers or workers with personal challenges may feel that they should be protected because of their particular vulnerabilities and/or for consistency with the organization's social mission. All of these claims must be taken seriously and there is no single way of defining fairness or weighing one group's claims against another's. Rather, it is the *perception* of unfairness that can undermine an organization's resilience and must be addressed in any effective HR resilience strategy.

Finally, foresight is needed to ensure that HR decisions taken in the short term in order to navigate a crisis do not seriously damage the organization over the long term. Indeed, the HR literature, although not crisis-oriented per se, is consistent in its emphasis on the importance of *investing* in workforces for the long term rather than viewing people simply as interchangeable inputs to short-term production. The risks of myopic decision making can be manifested in several ways. For example, firings or layoffs of higher-paid senior workers might destroy institutional memory needed for strategic guidance or effective relationship-building over the longer term. Alienation of minorities can undermine an organization's ultimate ability to serve its various constituencies or to hire outstanding employees in the future. Alternatively, policies that share the burdens of cutbacks among all groups may ultimately build morale and solidarity, and strengthen the organization's core values, allowing it to better withstand future shocks, despite possible short-term limitations of this approach.

BOX 8.3   COUNCIL OF INTERNATIONAL PROGRAMS

The Council of International Programs (CIP) is a small nonprofit organization that promotes international understanding through professional development and cross-cultural exchange. CIP operates as a central hub coordinating a network of five community and branch offices across the United States which together with its alumni network (the Council of International Fellowship) operates in 30 countries. The COVID-19 pandemic had a major impact on CIP because the cessation of international travel and programming interrupted revenue derived from international program fees and from its program to help clients obtain visas. CIP employs three full-time staff, and contracts for additional staff services as needed. This arrangement enables CIP to save on health insurance benefits as well as adjusting staffing to short-run needs.

WORKFORCE ADJUSTMENT IN A CRISIS

The interplay of flexibility, fairness and foresight criteria converge when an organization needs to adjust its payroll and/or its workforce size and composition in a crisis situation, as CIP and GSNEO have done. The benefits and costs associated with alternative strategies for payroll reduction (or expansion) are summarized in Table 8.1. This table helps clarify the implicit tensions between short-run benefits achieved to navigate a crisis at hand through various strategies, and the implications and consequences for productivity and resilience over the long term.

RECONCILING CONFLICTING CRITERIA

Especially in a time of crisis, a nonprofit organization has to make difficult decisions, none harder than those involving its workforce. There are always trade-offs to be made between achieving flexibility, being fair, and being prescient or cognizant of future implications for organizational wellbeing and resilience. Two main principles should govern the process of making these trade-offs: (1) an incremental approach guided by *thinking at the margins* and (2) *prudence* in the decision process including *transparency* and *effective communication* about the reasoning behind decisions and the implications of those decisions. We consider thinking at the margins first.

An incremental approach to HR decision making by thinking at the margins sounds like it would be myopic, but it is not. An incremental approach can be taken to fleshing out both long- and short-term impacts, and successive incremental assessments and adjustments can lead to better long-term results. The trick is to think at the margins of any decision to best understand its implications along the multiple dimensions along which trade-offs may be required. The basic idea is to ask: If a policy were advanced in small measure to address one dimension (say flexibility), what would happen along the other dimensions of concern (fairness and foresightedness)? This approach can be applied to various alternative policies in order to compare their impacts in a comprehensive way. Moreover, a focus on small changes allows organizational leaders to make realistic assessments within the realm of their current experience rather than be wildly speculative or naively extrapolative into unfamiliar territory.

It could be argued that nonprofit decision makers have no time for incrementalism in a crisis. Consider, for example, the immediate decisions that many nonprofits made to cut payroll in the COVID-19 pandemic. There is no question that leaders sometimes have to make quick and possibly radical decisions, even the elimination of whole programs or service functions. However, analysis at the margins still applies. First, in non-crisis times, policies can be carefully crafted for the future by following this approach. Second, even in the midst of a crisis, decisions can be reasoned through using this logic. The point is to *think* incrementally at the margins and to engage in successive rounds of thinking until a satisfactory solution is reached, at least in principle, even if the organization cannot experiment with each incremental adjustment in practice (Young, Steinberg, Emanuele and Simmons, 2019).

The marginal analysis framework offers a common approach to a wealth of nonprofit crisis-related decisions including choosing among alternative policies for workforce reduction or expansion; decisions to alter the balance

Table 8.1   *Alternative payroll reduction strategies*

Strategy	Benefits	Costs	Fairness	Perspective
Layoffs	Long-run flexibility to restructure staff; short-run savings	Long-run recruitment costs; loss of human and social capital; short-run severance costs; loss of capacity	May target younger or minority workers unfairly; care required to avoid perceived discrimination	Disinvestment in the workforce risks a cycle of organizational decline, but also a possible opportunity for renewal. Must be managed sensitively and strategically
Furloughs	Retains workers on call when conditions improve; short-run savings	Less long-run flexibility to restructure or replace staff; short-term disruptions and loss of capacity	Depends on whether certain groups are targeted more than others	Potentially retains talent for the long term while attaining short-term savings
Pay cuts	Avoids staff reductions; good for morale if everyone is in it together; short-run savings	Staff stress if deep cuts needed; long-run extra compensation when conditions improve	Can be seen as unfair if all staff are not equally affected or if it is felt that higher salaried workers should sacrifice more	Across-the-board cuts might be seen as fair and easier to implement but strategic cuts, sensitively managed, could facilitate long-run workforce investment
Substitute volunteers for paid workers	Retains HR capacity; short-run and possibly long-run savings	Extra costs of volunteer administration; possible loss of long- and short-run effectiveness	Paid staff may see this as unfair; different group impacts if composition of volunteers differs from paid workers	Requires careful assessment of relative effectiveness of volunteers for different tasks and their interactions with paid staff; not appropriate for professional positions requiring special credentials
Consolidate positions	May achieve new efficiencies; short-run and possibly long-run savings	Loss of short-run effectiveness; possible loss of long-run capacity	Unfair if eliminated workers are disproportionately young, women or from particular ethnic, racial or other groups	Cross-training can enhance long-run capacity and flexibility, and motivate staff, but increasing workloads can also lead to dissatisfaction and burnout
Combination of the above	Combination of benefits above	Combination of costs above	Depends on net impact on various groups of concern	Use analysis at the margin to determine the best combination

between salaried, contract and volunteer workers; consolidation or differentiation of job responsibilities among workers; and deployment of staff between
on-site work and working at home. We recognize here the complexity of nonprofit workforces. In the scenarios described below, we abstract from the fact
that nonprofits employ many different kinds of staff, including professionals
in a variety of disciplines, administrators and service workers. Thus, thinking
at the margin requires leaders to identify in their own minds the particular
worker positions or categories that would be considered for each increment of
workforce adjustment. (This in turn may reflect a set of priorities that leaders
may have among alternative organizational programs, or particular constraints
stemming from government contracts or collective bargaining agreements.)

Consider each of these issues, keeping the guidance in Table 8.1 in mind:

A. Payroll reduction: alternatives include layoffs, furloughs, reductions in hours and reductions in pay. The question to ask at the margin is "what would be the impacts of achieving an incremental reduction of say $10,000 in payroll by following each of these alternatives?" By reflecting on managers' best information and knowledge in current circumstances, the following judgments might be reached:

- Layoffs would increase flexibility by reducing fixed costs but would damage long-term effectiveness through loss of key staff (foresightedness). Issues of fairness would be raised if those laid off have seniority or are primarily members of minority groups.
- Furloughs would achieve some flexibility in the short term, but long-term flexibility would be limited by failure to reduce the future fixed costs of permanent staff. Long-term effectiveness would be maintained, assuming the crisis can be navigated, staff loyalty is not lost and ways can be found to make payroll more flexible in the long run through hiring policies (foresightedness). Fairness could be an issue, depending on who was furloughed or how furloughs were distributed, and whether furloughs were voluntary.
- Reductions in hours would not achieve additional flexibility unless targeted to permanent salaried employees. Long-term effectiveness would be maintained because all staff would be retained and hours could be restored (foresightedness). Fairness would depend on how reduction of hours is implemented. Across-the-board reductions may be perceived as more fair.
- Reductions in pay could be perceived as fair if implemented across the board in a uniform way. Long-term effectiveness would be retained with the prospect of restoring pay cuts once the organization navigated the crisis (foresightedness). There would be no gain in flexibility as the basic cost structure would not be altered.

Suppose, on the basis of this analysis, managers ranked these alternatives in the following order of preference: reductions in pay, followed by reductions in hours, furloughs and layoffs. Accordingly, a policy could begin to take shape based on an initial across-the-board pay cut. However, this now puts the organization into a different state, from which further incremental adjustments can again be considered. For example, suppose another $10,000 cut must be considered. The same mode of analysis can be repeated, but perhaps with different answers. Senior management may decide that the next reduction should come from further reduction in hours (following similar logic as in the first cut), or it may decide on a different course of action; for example, that the second increment of cutting should come in the form of furloughs in order to retain more flexibility, even at the cost of some loss of fairness. In the latter case the policy will have evolved to contain both the initial cut in hours and the implementation of furloughs. This analysis at the margin can continue so long as additional increments of payroll reduction are desired to navigate the crisis, yielding some combination of the four alternative strategies. Finally, note that this analysis need not take place over an extended period of time. Indeed, it can be done all at once if necessary. Rounds of analysis at the margin can be successively undertaken within the same decision period, but this does require management to be able to *visualize* how the organization would be changed after each round of analysis.

B. The balance between salaried employees, part-time (hourly) workers and volunteers: Another avenue for payroll reduction could be to substitute part-time and volunteer workers for salaried staff. Alternatively, in a growth context, the question would be which mode to use to expand labor capacity. Note, this strategy would not apply to positions where professionals are required to have certain credentials that volunteers (and possibly part-time workers) are unlikely to have, or where such substitutions are considered inappropriate, as in the GSNEO case. Like workforce reduction decisions, substitution decisions are also best approached at the margin. For simplicity, consider adjustment of the balance between paid workers and volunteers. We can analyze this decision in terms of successive reductions and increases in each type of labor, as follows:

> A substitution of one full-time equivalent (FTE) volunteer for one FTE paid employee would increase flexibility to address a current or anticipated crisis by providing cost savings and eliminating a fixed cost. It could damage long-term organizational capacity and effectiveness by reducing institutional memory and eroding the skill and reliability level of the staff, and it could impose harm in terms of perceived unfairness by stirring resentment among paid workers who may feel unappreciated and undervalued by the organization.
> Based on this analysis, management may decide to make the substitution, determining that the marginal gain in flexibility is worth the modest losses in long-term effectiveness and morale. The same reasoning may continue for the next few increments, say another two or three substitutions of volunteers for paid staff. At some level, however, the management may determine that an additional gain in flexibility is not worth the mounting losses in long-term effectiveness and perceived unfairness. At this point, the marginal gains are offset by the marginal losses, and management would have settled on the resulting new combination of paid and volunteer staff.

C. Consolidation and differentiation of job responsibilities: A third avenue for payroll reduction is to consolidate or combine existing job descriptions; alternatively, in an expansion situation, the issue would be whether to increase responsibilities of existing staff or to create new positions. For simplicity, assume that positions would be consolidated when vacancies occur naturally from retirements or other expected developments, rather than explicit layoffs, or in an expansionary mode positions would be filled rather than left vacant. (Alternatively, if layoffs or potential new hiring are involved, the decision process in *A* above would be followed, after which position consolidations and cross-training can be considered.) This allows us to separate the consolidation effect from the effect of layoffs or new hiring. Thinking at the margin would follow the same logic as above:

Consolidation of two existing positions into one might have the following marginal effects: Flexibility to navigate a crisis might increase because of possible productivity gains and cost savings. Long-term effectiveness might decrease because staff could become overstretched and feel burdened by additional responsibilities. Perceptions of unfairness could increase as the position is unfilled and workloads increase, causing resentment among workers. Alternatively, investment in cross-training could offset capacity losses and increase longer-term staff productivity. (For example, see the case of Our Lady of the Wayside in Chapter 5.)

Again, management might decide that the consolidation of the two positions is worthwhile and would increase the organization's resilience. However, the same conclusion may not be reached for successive position consolidations. When the marginal benefits of combining another two positions are just offset by its negative impacts at the margin, management will have found the right level of staff consolidation.

D. Deployment of employees between on-site work and working from home: This decision has less to do with cost savings than evaluating changes in the composition and deployment of the workforce that could increase its productivity, both to cope with a current crisis and to be more cost-effective in the future. This too is a decision best analyzed at the margin, by considering one employee (or type of employee) at a time:

Allowing one employee to work from home may increase flexibility by reducing office costs and affording the employee more time and discretion to schedule and carry out her work. Long-term effectiveness may also increase if the change results in higher morale or effectiveness of workers or an expansion of the organization's ability to draw on a broader labor market for talent by taking advantage of the reach of new technology; however, this may be offset by loss of benefits from employee interaction in a physical office. Finally, fairness would be questioned if the option of off-site, on-line work is not offered to everyone.

Again, management may determine that this small change at the margin is worthwhile. However, moving more and more employees to off-site work may diminish the additional benefits gained in successive rounds (for example, the additional flexibility and morale) and increase the additional costs (losses of staff interaction, perceptions of unfairness as some workers feel left behind). When management determines that transfer of one more additional staff members to off-site work yields no net gain, it will have arrived at its most desirable balance of on-site and on-line workers. Finally, it is worth noting here that this balance point is likely to change over time as so-called "multimodal" work models become more common and effectively managed (Hooijberg and Watkins, 2021).

PRUDENCE IN HUMAN RESOURCE DECISION MAKING

Especially in a crisis situation, the manner in which HR decisions are made can be as important as the choices themselves. This is because mishandling of the process can impact the very issues that managers seek to address in pursuing resilience through improved deployment of the workforce. In particular, poor handling of HR decisions can impair flexibility, undermine long-term organizational integrity and effectiveness, and generate perceptions of unfairness. While the principles for making critical HR decisions espoused here are intuitive and should be understood by all nonprofit leaders, the decisions themselves can be difficult and the processes for implementing changes are sensitive for those affected. As with other facets of resilience planning and decision making, such as use of technology, developing systems of measurement or restructuring finances, as discussed in other chapters, engagement of outside expertise and professional consultation can be helpful for HR decision making.

As suggested in our review of key literature above, HR management in nonprofit organizations is particularly complex and multifaceted. Many factors go into the functioning of a healthy and ultimately resilient nonprofit organization including an organizational culture that values and respects staff and volunteers, involvement of workers in important organizational decisions, and organizational and leadership structures that motivate people and signal the importance of their needs and concerns (Young, 2021). Especially critical elements of successful organizational decision making to achieve resilience through nonprofit HR strategies include communication, transparency, teamwork and leadership.

Effective communication of decisions to those affected is important because it impacts all three requirements for resilience. Ineffective communication can undermine flexibility by sparking resistance to desired changes, especially if the reasoning behind the changes is misunderstood or if those affected feel they were not consulted. It undermines a sense of fairness for the same reasons. Moreover, the impacts can be long-term, undermining the morale of the workforce and hence its ability to pull together when the organization is under threat.

Part of good communication is transparency. Decisions made in the middle of the night or hidden from view will generate resentment and misinformation. Best to be completely clear and honest about how decisions are made and what their impacts are expected to be, and indeed to include those affected in the conversations leading up to them. Clearly, this process can be messy, and individual privacy must be respected. But this is a matter of paying now or paying later. Leadership that avoids transparency is likely to undermine the organization's resilience over the long term.

A good part of effective HR change management is working in teams and having a broad cross-section of members of the organization take ownership of the collective wisdom of the organization. In the short run, this can make the decision-making process more cumbersome and perhaps less flexible. But over time a well-designed team process can increase flexibility and a sense of fairness by providing the infrastructure to build consensus or at least mutual understanding between management, staff and volunteers.

As noted in Chapter 7, an organization's ability to innovate depends on transformative leadership. To a large extent, this extends to HR strategy as well. Effective leaders will communicate effectively with members of their workforce, be open and honest with them, and bring them onboard with the organization's long-term vision and plan for resilience. The people in a non-profit organization are its most precious resource and a fundamental source of its resilience and success (Young, 2021).

SUMMARY

People are the ultimate source of a nonprofit organization's resilience. A happy and productive workforce can best absorb the shocks of major crises and help ensure its strength over the long term. Nonetheless, building resilience and navigating crises commonly involve very difficult, often wrenching decisions, especially with respect to changes in the size and composition of the workforce. In a serious crisis, this may involve severe measures such as layoffs, furloughs, payroll reductions and position consolidations. Even in periods of growth, workforce size, compensation and deployment decisions are demanding, especially if the goal is to achieve long-term stability and the capacity to withstand future organizational challenges.

To address their critical HR decisions, nonprofit leaders must keep three criteria in mind: flexibility, fairness and foresight. Flexibility allows an organization to roll with the punches when the organization is challenged. Fairness ensures that members of the workforce are being appropriately treated relative to each other as they must absorb some of the costs of adjustment. Foresight means that HR decisions are made both in normal and difficult times to help ensure that the workforce maintains and builds its productivity, morale and motivation over the long run. Trade-offs among these criteria are often required in making particular HR decisions, such as adjusting the size and composition of the workforce. The logic of thinking at the margin can assist nonprofit leaders to make the best possible decisions of this kind. Finally, the process through which decisions about the workforce are made is as important as the decisions themselves. Good communications, transparency and teamwork are especially important.

REFERENCES

Brudney, Jeffrey L. (2016). "Designing and Managing Volunteer Programs," chapter 22 in David O. Renz and Robert D. Herman (eds), *The Jossey-Bass Handbook of Nonprofit Leadership and Management*, 4th Edition. Hoboken, NJ: John Wiley & Sons, pp.688–733.

Casselman, Ben (2021). "As Workers Gain Pay Leverage, Nonprofits Can't Keep Up." *New York Times*, December 23. www.nytimes.com/2021/12/23/business/economy/nonprofit-jobs-wage.html.

Eliasoph, Nina (2020). "What Do Volunteers Do?," chapter 25 in Walter W. Powell and Patricia Bromley (eds), *The Nonprofit Sector: A Research Handbook*, 3rd Edition. Stanford, CA: Stanford University Press, pp.566–578.

Hooijberg, Robert, and Michael Watkins (2021). "The Future of Team Leadership is Multimodal." MIT Report, February 9. https://sloanreview.mit.edu/article/the-future-of-team-leadership-is-multimodal/.

Leete, Laura (2006). "Work in the Nonprofit Sector," chapter 7 in Walter W. Powell and Richard Steinberg (eds), *The Nonprofit Sector: A Research Handbook*, 2nd Edition. New Haven, CT: Yale University Press, pp.159–179.

Lucassen, Jan (2021). *The Story of Work*. New Haven, CT: Yale University Press.

National Council of Nonprofits (2021). "Updated Analysis: The Scope and Impact of Nonprofit Workforce Shortages." National Council of Nonprofits Report, December 13. www.councilofnonprofits.org/sites/default/files/documents/nonprofit-workforce-shortages-report.pdf.

Ton, Zeynep (2014). *Good Jobs Strategy*. New York, NY: Houghton Mifflin Harcourt.

Ulrich, Dave, Jon Younger, Wayne Brockbank and Mike Ulrich (2012). *HR from the Outside In*. New York, NY: McGraw-Hill.

Watson, Mary R., and Rikki Abzug (2016). "Effective Human Resource Management: Nonprofit Staffing for the Future," chapter 22 in David O. Renz and Robert D. Herman (eds), *The Jossey-Bass Handbook of Nonprofit Leadership and Management*, 4th Edition. Hoboken, NJ: John Wiley & Sons, pp.597–638.

Young, Dennis R., Richard Steinberg, Rosemarie Emanuele and Walter O. Simmons (2019). *Economics for Nonprofit Managers and Social Entrepreneurs*. Cheltenham, UK and Northampton, MA: Edward Elgar Publishing.

Young, Mark S. (2021), *Bless Our Workforce*. N.p.: blessourworkforce.com.

Cartoon 9   *Anyone know a good solution?*

9. Entrepreneurship and resilience

Crises create opportunities that may allow organizations to survive conditions of stress, to recover from trauma and even to prosper in ways previously unanticipated. Crises are typically disruptive of normal operations, creating space for new initiatives that might not otherwise be considered or even feasible. These circumstances are reminiscent of the "creative destruction" that economist Joseph Schumpeter (1949) argued was the basis of successful capitalism. Without it, economies stagnate and innovation is suppressed; but if allowed to proceed, economies can remain vibrant and increasingly productive (Aghion, Antonin and Bunel, 2021).

By "creative destruction," Schumpeter was referring to new developments that upset existing markets and require tearing down old infrastructures and building new ones. History is strewn with examples of this dynamic capitalism. Railroads replaced freight transport by waterways, cars and trucks replaced horses and buggies, mass production undermined craft industries, computers relegated cash registers and adding machines to museums, digital photography replaced film cameras, and personal phones and electronic communications have undercut postal services. While such developments arguably constitute progress in terms of societal productivity and consumer welfare, they have also left substantial losses in their wakes, borne by those invested in older technologies or lifestyles.

The destruction created in crises is not generally constructive and almost never intentional. Still, like controlled burning in areas vulnerable to wildfires, it often clears room for new growth and development. Crises take their largest toll of organizations that are poorly managed or under-resourced, or simply not sufficiently forward-looking, permitting more effective ones to expand or replace them. Moreover, crises create demands for new services and technologies, which may represent improvements over older ways of doing things. The COVID-19 pandemic provided numerous nonprofit examples, including substitution of on-line and home delivery services for on-site provision; at-home employment of workers in place of on-site working arrangements; new demands for housing, food and other needs of displaced individuals and families; closures and contractions of organizations unable to pay their bills and maintain their operations; and expansions of foodbanks and mental health care programs.

No one would wish the onslaught of catastrophe as a means to improve the functioning of nonprofit organizations, but given their likelihood, crises do offer an opportunity to learn about new possibilities for building the capacities and effectiveness of these organizations. However, this requires that nonprofits learn to exploit creative destruction when they are presented with it. Schumpeter (1949) identified entrepreneurship as the key. In his view, entrepreneurs implement "new combinations" in the provision of goods and services. These combinations may entail new, more efficient ways of producing particular services, creating new organizations, providing services in new markets or indeed providing entirely new kinds of goods and services to address latent demands (or even demands that consumers did not even know they had!). While Schumpeter's ideas were addressed to the for-profit economy, they apply equally well to nonprofits (Young, [1983] 2013). The key to their implementation is the presence of a nonprofit or social variety of entrepreneurship to recognize opportunities and catalyze them into successful ventures.

NONPROFIT ENTREPRENEURSHIP

The classical idea of an entrepreneur is that of an individual who creates a new business in order to make money. However, entrepreneurship is really a process and a mindset that takes on a variety of forms and operates in diverse contexts. Individuals can pursue new combinations inside existing organizations (so-called intrapreneurship) as well as creating new organizations. Teams of individuals can, and commonly do, work together to create new combinations of programs and services. And entrepreneurs can be driven by a variety of motivations other than profit, as they commonly are, especially in the nonprofit sector (Young, [1983] 2013). From the viewpoint of resilience, it is important that a nonprofit organization can create a culture of opportunity so that potential entrepreneurial actors within its orbit are encouraged and supported in their efforts to find new ways of doing things in response to problems and opportunities created by the advent or threat of crises or by major economic and social change.

There is substantial evidence that nonprofit and social entrepreneurship often manifests itself in the creation of new organizations because existing organizations fail to accommodate the energies and ambitions of their own employees and stakeholders (Young, [1986] 2013). Organizations typically exhibit inertia in their routines, and immobility and inflexibility in their structures of authority, governance and decision making. Entrepreneurship, in contrast, requires flexibility, fluidity, autonomy, risk-taking and openness to new and innovative approaches. This conflict is as common in nonprofit organizations as in for-profit businesses and helps explain why so many socially motivated individuals seek to "set up their own nonprofits" rather than work within existing structures to pursue their ideas. Indeed, the contemporary culture of "social entrepreneurship" promotes this notion, perhaps at the expense of investment in existing nonprofit organizational infrastructure and operations. However, as in the cases of Living Resources, Evergreen Cooperatives (see Box 9.2) and other organizations cited in this book, nonprofits can accommodate and encourage entrepreneurship through flexible structures and a culture sympathetic to change.

Certainly, engagement in social entrepreneurship by idealistic, energetic, motivated and independently minded individuals who want to venture out on their own should not be discouraged. Much good work gets done this way. However, in terms of resilience, existing nonprofit organizations need to learn how to accommodate and indeed exploit entrepreneurial initiative in order to nurture and renew themselves, rather than accede to the status quo and concede entrepreneurial energy to other entities. Having a problem-solving, forward-looking, innovation-centered culture positions existing nonprofits to cope with the onset of crises and to anticipate and prepare for future changes and shocks.

BOX 9.2 EVERGREEN COOPERATIVES

Evergreen Cooperatives is a collaborative venture of four major "anchor institutions" – the Cleveland Foundation, Case Western Reserve University, University Hospitals and the Cleveland Clinic – in the University Circle area of Cleveland, Ohio. Its mission is to address poverty in the inner city by creating worker-owned enterprises to train, employ and provide equity to local residents. It began by creating new businesses that service the anchor institutions, including a laundry, an urban farm and a solar energy business. Before the COVID-19 pandemic it also created a program of purchasing qualified existing businesses from owners seeking to cash out and retire, so that these could be converted to worker-owned firms. While this program began slowly, the pandemic created an opportunity for Evergreen to accelerate its pace by offering owners purchase prices based on pre-pandemic performance of their businesses; that is, "pandemic-proof" transactions.

ENTREPRENEURIAL CULTURE AND CRISIS OPPORTUNITIES

How can existing nonprofits create an entrepreneurial culture for themselves? One model is the "learning organization" discussed in chapters 7 and 11, and implicit in other chapters. In particular, organizations must be open to technological innovation (Chapter 7); prudent risk-taking (Chapter 2); collaboration with other organizations (Chapter 10); measuring, assessing and correcting their own performance (Chapter 11); and certainly encouraging and rewarding their own employees and volunteers for their initiatives and innovative ideas (Chapter 8). More than this, they should be constantly scanning with an entrepreneurial mindset for new opportunities to strengthen their organizations both during crises and over the longer term.

In essence, entrepreneurship is about problem-solving. Crises magnify existing problems and create new ones, underlining the importance of an entrepreneurial culture. Consider the COVID-19 pandemic. Nonprofit organizations were faced with multiple new or exacerbated problems: How could they respond quickly to demands for new services such as food and housing insecurity, or to their clients' increased emotional and financial distress? How could they maintain operations in the face of lost revenue? How could they even function when their staffs could not come into the office? How could they provide services that heretofore required their clients or customers to visit their facilities on-site? How could they accommodate new demands such as childcare for essential workers? How could they help relieve the distress of families directly impacted physically, socially and economically by the virus? These were all problems to be solved by each organization in its own way, requiring an entrepreneurial approach that superseded standard operating procedures and established service programs and protocols. Moreover, these problems often required "all hands on deck," so that ideas and talents of people throughout an organization could be harvested and nurtured. Entrepreneurial talent is not a monopoly of top management; nonetheless, leaders set the tone and create the environment in which the organization can benefit from entrepreneurial effort and initiative, wherever it resides in the organization and however it rises to the occasion.

In short, crises, and the threat of their onset, create special opportunities for nonprofit organizations to build their resilience. These opportunities are of several different types: First, crises can make extant "hard decisions" that the organization faces easier to identify and address, by magnifying and highlighting their importance. Second, crises may draw attention to organizational assets that are underutilized but might be employed to generate new resources or solve problems (as noted in Chapter 4 and discussed further below). Third, crises may create demands in the marketplace to which the organization may be well positioned to respond. For example, see the cases of Evergreen Cooperatives and the Jewish Community Center of Greater Pittsburgh (see Box 9.3). All these opportunities in turn require organizations to carefully scrutinize themselves and re-examine their competitive environments to assess how best to respond in a manner that ensures their future viability.

HARD DECISIONS

It is a natural tendency of organizations (as in contentious politics or everyday life) to "kick the can down the road"; that is, to postpone difficult decisions rather than face up to them. Nonprofits may shelter some operations and services that are ineffective or loss-making, because of sentimentality or loyalty to the organization's historical mission and traditions. Gift shops or fundraising events that run losses illustrate the point. Such operations may provide satisfaction to long-time volunteers or good memories or experiences for donors. But if these incidental benefits do not exceed the economic cost, a crisis can be a chance to phase them out and perhaps replace them with something more effective. More generally, a crisis may provide a special opportunity to examine an organization's entire portfolio of services, in terms of both their economic viability and the impact they have towards accomplishing the organization's mission (Oster, 2018). Building profitable and effective services and phasing down those that are loss-making or ineffective (or both) may offer an unanticipated benefit from a crisis.

Similarly, staffing arrangements can be re-examined in a crisis, which may be an opportunity to consolidate positions and even phase out or redirect unproductive workers, teams or departments. As Chapter 8 explains, such people-centric issues can be wrenching, and attention must be paid to fairness and recognition of meritorious service, but a crisis can make it clearer why effectiveness must be prioritized over sentimentality. Indeed, this consideration applies to the whole organization from top to bottom. Organizations that have been reluctant to address leadership and board turnover, for example, may find that a crisis offers the chance to face up to the challenges of refreshing the organization. Indeed, a period of crisis may even require a different sort of leadership than an organization has historically engaged. For example, an argument can be made that in the future nonprofit organizations are likely to require leaders with crisis-navigation skills more than they have in the past.

In terms of resilience, there is some irony in exploiting crises to address hard decisions that will ultimately improve a nonprofit organization's performance. The inefficiencies built up by historical inattention to these decisions constitute a form of organizational slack that can buffer an organization from the impacts of crises, so long as those inefficiencies are identified and reduced when crises actually occur. Thus, hard decisions require not only the reduction of inefficiencies but also the retention of buffers so that the organization is prepared for future crises. New staffing patterns should allow for some flexibility and redundancy, and new programming should reflect some diversification to buffer against change in future economic and social conditions.

UNDERUTILIZED ASSETS

Many nonprofit organizations have nonfinancial assets that they do not fully utilize for financial gain or mission fulfillment. Such assets can also be thought of as a form of slack, potentially available for relief and sustenance in a crisis. Nonprofit leaders with entrepreneurial mindsets naturally gravitate towards such assets, asking themselves how they can be used in new and better ways to advance the interests of the organization. In a crisis, this question becomes central and critical.

As noted in Chapter 4, underutilized assets can take the form of material assets, human resources and social assets. In the first instance, nonprofits with substantial real estate, unique buildings and grounds, or valuable collections of art or artifacts, can ask themselves if these assets can be further exploited to generate net income or additional mission impacts. Thus, botanical gardens can make themselves available in the off hours to special events, private parties and media companies. Museums can host corporate meetings and circulate the art they have in storage to other institutions or even individuals such as major donors. Universities can provide dorm space to tourists and other visitors.

Environmental organizations can offer excursions on their research vessels, and youth organizations can rent their campgrounds to families and organizations seeking short vacation stays or retreats for their staff in the off season. Of course, in a crisis organizations can also consider selling some of their underutilized assets (see Chapter 4), although this is problematic where these assets are still required for mission-related work, or otherwise restricted. Thus, a youth organization might want to sell some but not all of its acreage, unless it planned to disband its camping program. And a museum must be circumspect about selling donated works of art.

Similarly, nonprofits whose staffs have special expertise or celebrity value can, within the limits of availability, deploy these assets for public lectures and performances that can promote the organization's mission and also generate income, either directly through box-office fees or by stimulating additional donations. Scientists and curators can give public lectures, for example, and professors can teach in profitable executive education programs outside their mainstream, degree-related coursework.

Finally, many organizations have built "social capital" with other organizations in their communities and resource and service networks, which may serve narrow purposes but may be capable of doing more. Entrepreneurial initiative within such networks can unleash new potential through the initiation of collaborative efforts. For example, the Nonprofit Academic Centers Council (NACC) is an association of university academic centers originally established to facilitate exchange of information among nonprofit center leaders in member universities. But the members discovered that they could do more together, including the promulgation of common educational standards for their coursework, and sponsoring research on nonprofit management education. In a crisis, members of NACC can gather their collective wisdom, if not material help, to see them through. Larger nonprofit federations such as the Girl Scouts USA or the Jewish Community Centers Association of North America serve this purpose for their members and may even occasionally share staff capacity or other resources.

No nonprofit organization wants to maintain assets that are not well utilized, but the degree of such underutilization may not be understood until a crisis ensues. In normal times, no organization will utilize its assets to the fullest extent, nor should it necessarily seek to do so. A margin of slack in asset use serves as a protection held in reserve for difficult times. However, an entrepreneurial mindset will help an organization identify potentials for further asset utilization that can be productively engaged in good times and potentially redirected when crises loom.

RESPONDING TO NEW DEMANDS

As noted, crises can rearrange the economic landscape for nonprofits. Demand for some services may collapse, as it did for on-site arts performances in the pandemic. Demand for other services may increase, as they did for homeless and mental health services or foodbanks in recent economic recessions. And demands for whole new services may arise, such as day care for older children of essential workers who required assistance with on-line instruction while their parents worked during the pandemic. In these circumstances, an entrepreneurial nonprofit faced with declining demand for some of its services will try not just to stop the bleeding but will also assess how it can "pivot" towards new demands that fit its mission and capabilities. Thus, schools and performing arts organizations in the pandemic discovered demands for new forms of on-line presentation of their content as they coped with shutdowns of on-site performance or instruction. Similarly, foodbanks and social service organizations moved to home delivery of their services in place of on-site service and distribution.

Such pivoting is not easy and often not possible. It requires that new demands be within the purview of existing organizational missions and capacities. Those education and performance arts organizations with sufficient technological capacity could move on-line, and sometimes create new variants of their existing repertoires. But schools and museums did not undertake food distribution or homeless services, despite those new demands. The entrepreneurial mindset requires an assessment of *competitive advantage* that determines if one's own organization is best suited to address the new demands and will not lose the competition to other better positioned organizations.

BOX 9.3   JEWISH COMMUNITY CENTER OF GREATER PITTSBURGH

During the COVID-19 pandemic, the Jewish Community Center of Greater Pittsburgh (JCC) discovered that many of its members and others in the community were essential workers required to be away from home during the day while their children struggled with remote learning when their schools switched from on-site to on-line instruction. The JCC determined that it could extend its current day care services to school-age children and provide them with oversight and bandwidth for connections to their schools, in order to meet the new demands on their parents. This new revenue stream also helped the organization to overcome losses to its mainstream fitness and community services during the pandemic.

ENTREPRENEURSHIP AND SLACK

Entrepreneurship has a double-barreled relationship to resilience management in nonprofit organizations. On the one hand, the entrepreneurial mindset allows an organization to identify the opportunities for new combinations that will help the organization weather a crisis or position it better for future crises. This frequently involves identifying slack in the form of underutilized assets and turning it towards new, additional productive uses. It also involves identifying new, extant demands which the organization can productively address within its comfort zone of mission and skill sets. Organizations with a strong entrepreneurial culture will always try to "push the envelope" whether in crisis or not. But an extreme form of entrepreneurialism may not best serve the goal of resilience. As we have discussed throughout the book, not only is some level of slack or reserve healthy and necessary for response to challenges but eliminating slack through intense entrepreneurship can potentially make an organization fragile and more vulnerable. Organizations can "spread themselves too thin" by pursuing too many entrepreneurial opportunities without restraint.

This leads to the paradoxical conclusion that entrepreneurship is itself an important asset or capacity that requires a degree of reserve. Nonprofit leaders carry out many different functions in addition to finding new combinations, and that is as it should be. The Goldilocks rule applies here as well. Nonprofit leadership needs to be entrepreneurial and should be capable of shifting into entrepreneurial mode when opportunities arise and/or crisis threatens, but it should not be so intensively or pervasively entrepreneurial as to precipitate crises itself or leave the organization more vulnerable to future threats.

SUMMARY

The importance of an entrepreneurial mindset and organizational culture is not confined to crisis situations or preparing for catastrophe. A healthy nonprofit organization will always be looking for creative ways to solve problems and serve its mission in better ways. However, crises can offer special opportunities in the wake of the creative destruction they may precipitate. For example, crises may block an organization from pursuing its routine agenda and require it to "pivot" to new combinations or ways of doing its work. Or they may create new demands and funding opportunities for services to its traditional clientele. While entrepreneurship is commonly associated with heroic individuals creating their own new organizations, it is primarily entrepreneurship internal to organizations, or intrapreneurship, that serves to build a nonprofit's resilience by finding new possibilities to carry on its work and to respond to new opportunities in the community. In pursuit of entrepreneurial resilience, nonprofits can draw on important facets of organizational slack, including underutilized assets and latent entrepreneurial capacities of its leadership and staff. In doing so, they should seek to exploit such slack in a crisis and maintain a prudent margin of slack in normal times.

REFERENCES

Aghion, Philippe, Celine Antonin and Simon Bunel (2021). *The Power of Creative Destruction*. Cambridge, MA: Belknap Press.
Oster, Sharon M. (2018). "Product Diversification and Commercial Ventures," chapter 13 in Bruce A. Seaman and Dennis R. Young (eds), *Handbook of Research on Nonprofit Economics and Management*, 2nd Edition. Cheltenham, UK and Northampton, MA: Edward Elgar Publishing, pp.269–284.
Saidel, Judith R., and Elizabeth A.M. Searing (2020). "Public Agency Strategies, Collaborative Contracting and Medicaid Managed Care." *Perspectives on Public Management and Governance*, 3(3), 239–255.
Schumpeter, Joseph A. (1949). *The Theory of Economic Development*. Cambridge, MA: Harvard University Press.
Young, Dennis R. [1983] (2013). *If Not for Profit, for What?* Lexington, MA: Lexington Books. https://scholarworks.gsu.edu/facbooks2013/1/.
Young, Dennis R. [1986] (2013). *Casebook of Management for Nonprofit Organizations.* https://scholarworks.gsu.edu/facbooks2013/2/.

Cartoon 10   That's what friends are for

10. Networks and resilience

BOX 10.1 JEWISH COMMUNITY CENTERS ASSOCIATION OF NORTH AMERICA

Most of the 171 Jewish Community Centers Associations of North America (JCCA/NA) effectively closed their doors to on-site programming during the early months of the COVID-19 pandemic. Given that earned income represents approximately 80% of operating revenue for these organizations, closures presented a major threat to their survival. Through several separate initiatives, Jewish charitable networks helped to provide a safety net to assist these organizations through the crisis. The JCCA/NA developed a four-part program of information-sharing, collaboration on (virtual) programming, communication, and social and emotional support for the workforce through its JResponse program. Eight major national Jewish charitable organizations, including the JCCA/NA, formed an Emergency Pandemic Coalition to ensure that financial aid continued to support critical services. And the UJA-Federation in New York provided $10 million to 22 JCCs in the New York region.

Few if any nonprofit organizations operate in a vacuum. By and large, nonprofits work in the context of multiple networks of service suppliers, resource providers, advocacy associations, regulators and other organizations that interface with, and contribute to, their operations. Indeed, a substantial fraction of nonprofits in the United States are autonomous or semi-autonomous members of formal federations or franchise systems, like the Jewish Community Centers (JCCs) in Box 10.1 or Girl Scout Councils, chapters of the American Red Cross, local United Ways or members of the American Association of Museums. While associations, federations and less formal networks of nonprofits serve multiple purposes, including policy advocacy, standard-setting and skills training, their role in underwriting the resilience of nonprofit organizations is equally important (even if less appreciated).

MANY VARIETIES OF NONPROFIT NETWORKS

Formal federations and franchise systems are one end of a rich spectrum of nonprofit networks, ranging from very informal and ad hoc sets of inter-organizational connections to highly centralized formal systems. Nor are these networks restricted to nonprofit organizations themselves. For example, Koliba (2015) described five broad categories of nonprofit networks involved in the governance and public policy aspects of nonprofit operations: grant and contract networks, partnership networks, advocacy networks, intergovernmental networks and regulatory networks. Nonprofits play different kinds of roles in these networks, including grantees and contractors, partners with other organizations in the network, peers of other member organizations, objects (for example, fund recipients or regulated entities) of network activity and third-party regulators. Overall, networks represent interdependence among network members; thus, it is the *relationships* that develop among network members that underwrite the potential for increasing the resilience of network members as well as the network itself.

Aside from inter-sectoral networks, there is also a wide variety of formal network arrangements among nonprofits themselves. Young and Faulk (2018) describe a spectrum from highly decentralized associations to centralized corporate structures, including a wide array of federated structures that balance local member autonomy and central control. The fact is, however, that nonprofits are almost certain to belong to several networks at the same time, each with a different structure and purpose. Moreover, nonprofit networks continue to evolve as needs change and nonprofits reassess their requirements from year to year. In many cases, nonprofits have choices as to what networks they will join, what networks no longer serve their purposes, and what new networks may need to be formed, formally or otherwise. Should they join or renew their membership in this or that professional or trade association? Should they become a part of a policy advocacy network? Should they seek to enter a grantees' or contractors' network associated with a particular foundation or government agency? Should they organize their own collaborative network? As a general rule, belonging to multiple and substantial networks serves nonprofits well in terms of their resilience. There are multiple reasons for this, as discussed in the following sections.

NETWORKS AND SOCIAL CAPITAL

As noted in Chapter 4, the relationships between members of a network constitute "social capital," part of the "soft capital" that is an important component of organizational assets, analogous to the physical, financial and human resource assets that all organizations require to do their work. Just as buildings and equipment, financial reserves and staff expertise underwrite the ability of organizations to provide their goods and services, social capital supports the interfaces between an organization and external agents on which it depends, including other organizations with which it may collaborate, as well as suppliers, regulators, funders and consumer and client groups. Moreover, the relationships themselves may form a kind of "safety net" for helping members of a network when they face difficulties and challenges. In the COVID-19 pandemic, members of federations had a common interest in policies and practices that would enable organizational survival and continued operation. Charitable and governmental funders of nonprofits in various fields also had a stake in the continued viability of their grantees. Thus, networks associated with foundations, federations and government funders convened to find ways of helping out in a crisis. In Cleveland, Ohio for example, major local foundations and United Way collaborated through contributions to a special fund to help vulnerable local nonprofits survive the pandemic. In Cleveland and elsewhere, being a part of these funding networks was an important way for vulnerable local nonprofits to weather the storm. In the aftermath of the attacks on the World Trade Center in New York in 2001, affected local nonprofits that belonged to networks were better able to recover than those that were not, for a variety of reasons including direct access to funding as well as better information about sources of assistance (Abzug and Derryck, 2002). Such networks implicitly served the purpose of external resource reservoirs and safety nets that could be looked to for help.

The social capital embedded in nonprofit networks can be leveraged in nonfinancial forms of assistance in a crisis. Within federation structures, for example, information and expertise can be shared and common approaches to similar challenges developed, as the JResponse program did for JCCs in the pandemic. Moreover, stronger members of a network can assist weaker ones in a crisis through consultations and sharing of expertise and other resources. This is especially true in networks such as the JCCs or Girl Scouts, where leaders of individual member organizations meet together for annual conferences and educational programs, and where new leaders of these organizations are recruited from a common pool of upper-level managers nationwide. In these circumstances, close relationships are likely to develop among leaders of member organizations, which can be tapped for help and collaboration in a crisis.

It is worth considering also that nonprofit networks contribute to the resilience of their member organizations by helping them to become more knowledgeable in various ways; that is, to develop as "learning organizations" (see chapters 7, 9 and 11). A decentralized network of similar member organizations, such as the JCC Association or the League of American Orchestras, can be thought of as a "natural experiment" in a crisis situation. Each member will necessarily experiment with different solutions to common problems. One organization may try to use furloughs to adjust its workforce while another may try across-the-board pay reductions, for example. Members will experiment with different forms of on-line activity to replace on-site services, and so on. The value of the network is that it helps members compare notes, evaluate results and determine implications for their own local circumstances. A central node in the network – for example, a federation or association head-quarters – may be helpful in systemizing this information and disseminating it to members in a timely fashion. Many nonprofit networks surveyed their members during the pandemic and shared findings to assist them. The same was true of specialized networks or membership organizations such as the Nonprofit Finance Fund, Candid, the National Council of Nonprofits and Philanthropy Ohio, which conducted their own general surveys and shared results with members as well as with the public at large.

NETWORKS, FIXED VERSUS VARIABLE COSTS, AND ECONOMIES OF SCALE AND SCOPE

In Chapter 5 we discussed how conversion of fixed to variable costs could help an organization become more resilient, because variable costs can be trimmed to reflect crisis-induced reductions in output and corresponding losses of revenue, while fixed cost must be maintained in the short run, until they can be restructured. Networks can assist with this strategy in some circumstances. If, for example, a central node of a network (call it a headquarters) can take on certain functions such as purchasing or personnel recruitment, then individual member organizations need not maintain the corresponding staff infrastructure. Rather, members can purchase the service as needed, from the central node, a variable cost that varies with an organization's activity level. Since most members of such a network will have need for such services, though not all at once, the central node may be better positioned to weather any disruptions from a crisis, smoothing over the volatile changes experienced by individual members. This is analogous to the use of cloud computing as an alternative to storing files and programs on individual computers. A network can sustain a cloud when a crisis rains on its members, without members having to suffer the fixed costs of cloud maintenance.

A related benefit of networks is their potential to help members achieve economies of scale and scope, also discussed in Chapter 5. If members can combine some of their operations, as in the examples cited above, and if operation at larger scale results in lower average costs, then members can share the savings. This may be manifested through production by a central node, as in the example above, or through other collaborative arrangements such as close coordination of operations by the member organizations. For example, a social service agency specializing in residential care may require certain counseling and assessment services as well as community placements for some of its clients, while another agency specializing in preventive and community services may occasionally require residential care for some of its clientele. Coordination of case management might achieve this interface more effectively and at a lower cost than maintaining separate systems.

But should nonprofit organizations not be exploiting these potential economies on a regular basis, regardless of the threat or onset of a crisis? Possibly, but it is the *potential* for such arrangements that constitutes the slack or reserve that organizations in a network can fall back on in a crisis. Thus, planning for arrangements that can exploit such economies in a network is an effective form of crisis preparation. Moreover, the options for moving in this direction, combined with the capacity or necessity to maintain the status quo in the short run, offer organizations in a network an additional level of flexibility for navigating a crisis.

REDUNDANCY, RECIPROCITY AND ROBUSTNESS

If networks are thought of simply as sets of connections between a certain number of members (nodes) then clearly there are numerous ways in which those connections can be made; that is, how the network itself can be structured. In particular, connections can be simple and sparse, with relatively few pathways from one node to another, or they can be dense, with multiple pathways connecting members to one another. Moreover, networks can be more or less "egalitarian," either concentrating connections in certain nodes (hubs) or spreading the connections out evenly among members. For example, a network can feature all members connected to a central hub but not directly to one another, or no hub at all, with multiple direct connections among members.

The analysis of networks is the stuff of highly technical systems such as airline route planning and telecommunications infrastructure. Such analyses are usually efficiency-oriented, focused on determining how travel or messaging through a network can be arranged to minimize costs or maximize traffic. Networks have also been the subject of substantial social science scholarship in connection with understanding the operations of organizations and markets, including issues of control, competition, collaboration and communication in these realms (see, for example, Nohria and Eccles, 1992). Network structure is critical to nonprofit resilience management as well, both for members of a network and for networks as a whole. A key question is: What are the principles to be kept in mind by nonprofit organizations seeking to build or join networks to foster their resilience? A related question is how can networks themselves – for example, federations or associations of nonprofits – build their own resilience? Three dimensions of networks are critical to addressing these challenges: redundancy in network relationships, reciprocity associated with links in networks, and the robustness or size and density of the network as a whole.

Redundancy

An important theme in this book is that multiple means and capacities under-pinning the operations of nonprofit organizations can be a good thing, not necessarily wasteful and often helpful in ensuring resilience. Holding assets in reserve, diversifying sources of income and overlapping staff competencies illustrate the point. The same is true for networks. If good relations with one local funder is good, for example, having good relations with two or more is better. More generally, having multiple channels for obtaining key informa-tion, securing critical resources, pursuing advocacy goals, developing collab-orative partnerships, or reaching clients and consumers is a strength that helps insulate an organization from disruptions to any one link in the network. There are limits, of course, to the degree of redundancy that is desirable in any given circumstance. In particular, the quality of inter-organizational relationships is very important, especially whether those relationships can be counted on in a crunch. In a world of resource scarcity nonprofits must necessarily focus on those connections that are most critical, necessarily limiting the number of network relationships they can productively cultivate and simultaneously maintain.

BOX 10.2   THE NATIONAL TRUST

As Europe's largest conservation charity, the National Trust is responsi-ble for the preservation and operation of over 500 historic houses, castles, parks and gardens, 100,000 acres of land and 780 miles of coastline in the United Kingdom (www.nationaltrustannualreport.org.uk). In addition to its individual members the Trust also partners with a variety of corporate sponsors with which it works on media and communications, environmen-tal, organic food, horticultural and therapeutic and recreational projects. The Trust's revenues derive largely from memberships, which constituted 43% of its income in 2019, and various forms of earned income, including admission fees, rental income and enterprises such as gift shops and con-cessions, which constituted another 44%. The remaining income came from gifts, grants and investment income. The COVID-19 pandemic led to substantial losses of earned income, reducing the Trust's total operat-ing revenue by almost a quarter between 2020 and 2021 and necessitat-

ing major cost reductions. However, membership income grew to record levels in 2020 and continued to hold steady in 2021. This was achieved in part through an advertising campaign that energized the Trust's membership network and capitalized on the public's growing desire for enjoying the outdoors and empty spaces during the pandemic (Hall, 2021).

Reciprocity

Nonprofit network relationships can be thought of as one- and two-way streets. One-way streets may not be very helpful in a crisis. Unless a connection to a person or another organization in the network is reciprocal in some way, that other party is less likely to be of help in a crisis situation. This is an important consideration for nonprofits seeking to build their network resilience. To paraphrase John F. Kennedy, nonprofit organizations need to ask not only what their partners can do for them, but what they can do for their partners.

The other side of the transaction can be explicit or implicit. Links to a funder promise future resources, and links to a regulator or information provider may allow more sympathetic understanding and treatment in regulatory and evaluation processes. But from the viewpoint of the nonprofit reaching out to build its network, careful thought should be given to how to reciprocate in these relationships; for example, by volunteering on committees or providing insightful information that the funder or evaluator might not otherwise have. In building their networks, the National Trust and Dress for Success (see Box 10.3) brought their special capacities to the table: The Trust drew on its access to open spaces and nature during the pandemic to appeal to potential members, while Dress for Success could provide job market assistance to laid-off workers of its corporate partners.

The importance of reciprocity is more obvious in networks that involve partnerships among peers. Collaborating with peers is clearly a two-way street, otherwise there is little reason to participate. Each partner must perceive a benefit to its own organization. If the collaboration is productive in this fashion, then the relationship can also serve as a reservoir of trust and mutual understanding to be called upon in a crisis. If there is no reciprocity the link will be fallow, and less likely to be helpful in an emergency. To go a bit further, network relationships can take on the character of political chits, if some organizations feel beholden to others and hence obligated to respond when called upon. There is, however, a potential contradiction in this situation: If two organizations in a partnership within a network seek to position themselves as the party to whom something is owed, then neither may be so viewed by the other. Still, strong reciprocal relationships may be built that can create a reservoir of trust and obligations for future exigencies.

The importance of reciprocity also holds within structured networks such as member associations and federations in the relationships between local members and a central node such as a corporate headquarters. The character of this reciprocity will vary with the particular association or federation structure. Highly centralized organizations such as the American Cancer Society can more easily dictate the terms of trade between headquarters and local chapters. Unless a certain local chapter is especially powerful because of its size and local roots, it may have little leverage over headquarters. In a less hierarchical situation, such as Dress for Success or the JCCs, which are locally autonomous and separately incorporated, there is a reciprocal relationship between members and headquarters. Such federations are more like trade associations in which members pay dues and belong voluntarily and where the national association is seen as a servicer of members' needs. In this case, headquarters needs the help of members as much as members need the support of headquarters. Thus, for both the individual member organization and for headquarters, building of mutual trust is a way of building resilience. In a crisis that threatens headquarters, member organizations will be more likely to come to its support, and in a local crisis headquarters is more likely to come to the aid of a member organization.

Federations highlight the relationship between redundancy and reciprocity. Member organizations in a centralized federation will have fewer network options as these are likely to be controlled or limited by headquarters. In decentralized federations, members may have the option of joining other associations and even the right to leave the federation itself. In the latter case, there is more opportunity to build resilience through redundancy, although reciprocity in member–headquarters links remains important as well.

Robustness

A well-known characteristic of networks is that, if left to proliferate organically, their interconnections increase exponentially with the number of nodes or members. This gives rise to "network economies" that make larger networks more economical than smaller ones (more contacts per node). Network economies help explain the success of social media and internet companies, and are a reason that just a few large companies are able to dominate the field. For the individual user, the bigger the network, the better, if what is sought is access to a wider world of information.

BOX 10.3 DRESS FOR SUCCESS OF NORTHERN NEW JERSEY

The mission of Dress for Success is to "empower women to achieve economic independence by providing a network of support, professional attire and the development tools to help women thrive in work and in life." Dress for Success of Northern New Jersey (DFSNNJ) is one of 142 affiliates of Dress for Success Worldwide (DFSWW), which provides financial oversight and guidance to members in addressing the mission. Before the COVID-19 pandemic, DFSNNJ also built a local network of partner organizations, including social service agencies that referred clients, and corporate partners that offered funding, recognition and volunteers. In addition, DFSNNJ worked with local churches and colleges, forming satellite programs to recruit women as clients and volunteers. When the pandemic hit, DFSNNJ's network of referring agencies closed down and clients were left at home without childcare or transportation options. Corporate and university partners were also laying off or furloughing workers and one-time volunteers were becoming potential clients. In response, DFSNNJ, led by its Executive Director Kim Iozzi, asked its network partners how it could assist them. This outreach helped keep the network connected and led DFSNNJ to re-orient itself to on-line provision, including career-building services for former volunteers; meanwhile, DFSNNJ's corporate partners shifted their support from helping with in-person events to funding webinars and Amazon wish lists. As a result, in 2020, DFSNNJ engaged 490 new women as clients, 42% more than the year before.

For nonprofits choosing to join networks or interested in growing their own networks, the issues surrounding network size are more nuanced. Becoming parts of larger networks certainly does increase access to a wider number of potential peers, partners and supporters. For purposes of resilience, that is nominally a good thing. Fishing in the ocean has more potential than fishing in a pond. Larger networks offer more redundancy for seeking help in a crisis or for partnering to build resilience in advance of a crisis. Thus, as a member of a global federation, Dress for Success of Northern New Jersey (DFSNNJ) had access to peers worldwide. But the quality of network relationships can be just as important as the number of relationships, as our discussion of reciprocity indicates, and as DFSNNJ's initiative in building its local network illustrates. Thus, being selective about what networks to join and how much to build out an organization's own networks hinges on an organization's assessment of the trust, dependability and mutual reliance that has been built into its network relationships. Given that it takes time, energy and focus to cultivate productive network relationships, it is unlikely that maximizing network size is the best guarantor of resilience. Here again, the Goldilocks philosophy comes into play. Resilience is not well served by networks that are too sparse, nor is it well served by immersing in multiple, large networks unless one is selective in cultivating productive links into a subnetwork customized for the organization's particular needs. Thus, a network that is not too dense but not too sparse, where links are not just one-way but also not superficial, constitutes the network that may be just right.

STRONG AND WEAK TIES

Issues of redundancy, reciprocity and robustness have been studied by sociologists wishing to understand how relationships among people within an organization influence the efficacy of the organization itself (see Nohria and Eccles, 1992, for example). A key distinction is made in this literature between so-called "weak" and "strong" ties between individuals or organizations in a network. Strong ties are connections that involve significant time, intensity of interaction, intimacy and reciprocity, whereas weak ties are less intense along these various lines. Mark Granovetter, a pioneer in network theory, summed up the difference as follows (Granovetter, 1983, quoted in Krackhardt, 1992): "Weak ties provide people with access to information and resources, beyond those available in their own social circles; but strong ties have greater motivation to be of assistance and are typically more easily available." Earlier Granovetter (1973) had argued that weak ties can be more important than strong ties because "a weak tie is likely to provide new information from disparate parts of the system," whereas information from strong ties is "more likely to be redundant"; thus, strong ties would "not be a channel for innovation" (Krackhardt, 1992, p.216). But from a resilience point of view, involving organizations in networks, we can see that *both* strong and weak ties are important.

Nonprofits tend to have strong ties to funders in their networks, and to headquarters and perhaps fellow organizational members of a federation of which they may be a part. They may have miscellaneous weak ties to other organizational members in professional and trade associations, advocacy coalitions and community groups. The strong ties are likely to be reciprocal and more intense, and the information and support from other members of such networks will in fact be more redundant. From a resilience perspective this is a good thing; redundancy in funding and service networks means that in times of crisis, there are more possibilities for help. However, the weak ties will be more diverse, offering a variety of ideas and innovative solutions to solve difficult problems in a crisis. For example, a YMCA in a given location is more likely to receive help from its regional office and perhaps from fellow Ys in its locality, as well as local funders, and the more redundant these ties are, the better. But it is also more likely to learn of new practices and innovative solutions from its memberships in widespread networks such as national youth service, social justice, business management and child welfare associations, as well as through ad hoc relationships developed in professional conferences attended by the Y's leadership.

In short, resilience requires nonprofits to intensively cultivate both weak and strong ties, within a substantial panoply of networks relevant to their missions. These networks and ties require advance cultivation in good times, so that they can be counted on when crises erupt.

SUMMARY

Most nonprofits belong to multiple, diverse networks. These networks can be formal, such as federations or professional or trade associations, or informal and ad hoc networks created to address specific problems or issues. Networks provide opportunities for nonprofits to build social capital, and to achieve potential cost savings through economies of scale and scope. These networks are an important source of resilience because they offer various forms of assistance to nonprofits in challenging circumstances. In particular, network relationships, especially if they are sufficiently redundant, reciprocal and robust, can serve as reservoirs of support and even safety nets for individual network members. Nonprofit resilience requires nonprofits to engage in networks with both strong and weak ties. Strong ties can offer the slack resources on which nonprofits can draw in a crisis, while weak ties generate new ideas and information with which nonprofits can build their resilience strategies over time.

REFERENCES

Abzug, Rikki, and Dennis Derryck (2002). "Lessons from the Crisis: New York City Nonprofits After September 11." *Nonprofit Quarterly*, March 21. https://nonprofitquarterly.org/lessons-from-crisis-new-york-city-nonprofits-post-september-11/.

Granovetter, Mark S. (1973). "The Strength of Weak Ties." *American Journal of Sociology*, 78, 1360–1380.

Granovetter, Mark S. (1983). "The Strength of Weak Ties: A Network Theory Revisited", Sociological Theory, 1: 201–233.

Hall, Rachel (2021). "Record Numbers Join National Trust Despite Claims of 'Anti-Woke' Critics." *The Guardian*, October 29. www.theguardian.com/uk-news/2021/oct/29/record-numbers-join-national-trust-despite-claims-of-anti-woke-critics.

Koliba, Christopher J. (2015). "Civil Society Organization Accountability within Governance Networks," chapter 5 in Jean-Louis Laville, Dennis R. Young and

Philippe Eynaud (eds), *Civil Society, the Third Sector and Social Enterprise*. London: Routledge, pp.91–108.

Krackhardt, David (1992). "The Strength of Strong Ties: The Importance of *Philos* in Organizations," in Nitin Nohria and Robert G. Eccles (eds), *Networks and Organizations*. Boston, MA: Harvard Business School Press, pp.216–239.

Nohria, Nitin, and Robert G. Eccles (eds) (1992). *Networks and Organizations*. Boston, MA: Harvard Business School Press.

Young, Dennis R., and Lewis Faulk (2018). "Franchises and Federations: The Economics of Multi-site Nonprofit Organizations," chapter 15 in Bruce A. Seaman and Dennis R. Young (eds), *Handbook of Research on Nonprofit Economics and Management*, 2nd Edition. Cheltenham, UK and Northampton, MA: Edward Elgar Publishing, pp.300–322.

Cartoon 11   All hands on deck!

11. Red flags and stress tests

BOX 11.1   THE COMMUNITY HEALTH CENTER OF CAPE COD

The Community Health Center of Cape Cod (CHCCC) provides comprehensive health care services, regardless of ability to pay, to residents in the Cape Cod area of Massachusetts. It operates with an annual budget of approximately $20 million, two-thirds of which is supported by net patient service revenues. In the COVID-19 pandemic these revenues declined by 6% (approximately $1 million), a shortfall that was more than covered by increases in public and private grants, including a federal Paycheck Protection Program loan. Total revenues continued to grow in 2021. CHCCC prides itself on being "data-driven" in its management, which helped it to anticipate and adapt to the crisis and plan for future crises. Its 2020–2023 strategic plan helped shape its data management system, which includes metrics and dashboard displays for tracking the quality of patient outcomes, the organization's financial performance, and the performance of each of its operating divisions and medical providers (medical staff). The management of CHCCC credits its data management system for getting ahead of the crisis. In collaboration with the county government, CHCCC was able to track local COVID cases, facilitating early testing, treatment and later vaccination efforts, helping to reduce the local transmission of the disease. CHCCC's internal data system also highlighted increases in virtual medical visits with the onset of the pandemic, enabling timely expansion of its telemedicine program, which in turn helped staunch the loss of patient revenues.

Unlike certain businesses and industries, such as on-line retail and entertainment companies or professional sports leagues, nonprofit organizations are not especially well known for being data-driven in their management practices. However, managing for resilience in an era of crises now requires nonprofits in most fields of activity to become conversant with data collection, analysis and interpretation, so as to successfully prepare for and navigate the hazards they face. This data-analytic capacity has two parts: signals that *alert* the organization to imminent and developing crisis situations, and indicators that communicate whether the organization is *ready* to cope in those situations. These are two different but related functions that call for two different approaches: warning signals on the one hand, and safety checks and stress tests on the other.

A useful metaphor is driving a car. Road signs, traffic alerts, GPS and weather advisories provide warnings of dangers ahead, while dashboard lights and gauges signal whether the car and driver are headed for trouble because of internal issues. Is there enough gas? Is the engine running normally? Are tires properly inflated? Are you going too fast? Are your lights on? A driver needs all these signals to anticipate the onset of a crisis or to avoid or ameliorate one. Red flags are the blinking lights that go off on the dashboard when something is amiss.

However, the driver also needs to know whether the car is capable of navigating and surviving a crisis. Has the car been put through its paces before it is ever approved as roadworthy? Are inspections and maintenance schedules up to date? Has the car met requirements for oil changes, tire replacements and other regularly scheduled maintenance? Even more important, has the car (or its model) been sufficiently tested before leaving the factory? Race car drivers, factory mechanics and computer simulations do the stress tests on new models before they are sold to the general public.

Table 11.1   Monthly executive briefing illustration

Domain	Threat	Urgency	Vulnerabilities	Action
Nature/Environment	Summer storms	Likely; severe urgency	Loss of physical plant; loss of internet; loss of income from program shutdowns	Facility review and upgrades
Economic	Impending recession	Unlikely this year; mild concern	Loss of contributions and investment revenue	Monitor; build financial reserves
Social	Urban unrest	Possible this summer; moderately urgent	Increased demand for service; loss of contributions	Monitor closely; plan for staff expansion and special fundraising appeal
Internal	Staff burnout	High likelihood; serious concern	Loss of workforce; disruption of services; loss of earned income	Initiate staff discussions; review workloads; build volunteer capacity
Other	Terrorist attack	Unlikely; deadly impacts	Loss of assets; losses of morale and staff capacity; disruption of services and income	Review protocols; develop partnerships with other vulnerable agencies

The questions for nonprofits are: What kinds of road signs, dashboard signals and gauges do they need to warn of approaching crises, and what kinds of stress tests can determine their prospective resilience in navigating a crisis situation? These questions apply to all nonprofit organizations, no matter their size and sophistication. However, appropriate informational systems can and should be customized to the resource capacities and particular risk profiles of individual organizations. Below we suggest templates for dashboards, stress tests and monthly executive briefings. These tools are basically intended to monitor organizational and environmental conditions so that leaders are warned of impending crises and continuously informed about their organizational capacities to withstand them. Indeed, some organizations use the term "readiness" to describe the process. Such tools basically help nonprofit leaders *prepare* for crises or be ready for them, and to a degree they should be helpful in navigating a crisis once it erupts. In calmer periods, these tools are also useful for routine management purposes, because day to day a wise nonprofit manager will always be keeping an eye out for trouble. In general, these tools can be viewed as means for building resilient nonprofit organizations, but they are also defining features of organizations that maintain their resilience over time. The CHCCC case illustrates what a resilient organization can do to maintain its self-awareness. In contrast, the cases of Hull House (see Box 11.2) and FEGS (Box 11.3) demonstrate what can happen if a nonprofit is not so cognizant of its vulnerabilities.

BOX 11.2 HULL HOUSE

Hull House was one of the original settlement houses, co-founded in 1889 by social welfare pioneer Jane Addams as a resource for Chicago's most vulnerable citizens, especially immigrants. Over the next century, Hull House's scope grew to include multiple locations, client groups and a variety of social, legal and educational services. Hull House's funding also shifted dramatically from primarily private donor support to heavy reliance on revenues from government sources. Insufficiency and delays in government funding combined with the difficulties of maintaining multiple aging properties caused Hull House's liabilities to grow. In 2012, Hull House suddenly closed its doors. Had the management or the governing board been tracking the warning signs and metrics for the organization, this would not have been a surprise. Flynn and Tian (2014) illustrate what such a tracking system could have been for Hull House, revealing that revenues and expenses were both declining while multiple liabilities were building.

BOX 11.3   FEGS

In March 2015, the giant New York human services nonprofit known as FEGS (Federated Employment and Guidance Service) filed for bankruptcy. In analysis conducted afterwards, numerous problems emerged, including late payments for government contracts, insufficient funding to cover full costs, lack of funding to develop infrastructure and capacity, and many other vulnerabilities. Few of these problems should have been a surprise. Had adequate internal financial and programmatic reporting infrastructure been maintained, it could have provided an early warning about the dire straits that FEGS was in (Commission to Examine Nonprofit Human Services Organization Closures, 2016).

ROAD SIGNS, DASHBOARDS AND RED FLAGS

Nonprofits need *road signs* to warn them of the likelihood and consequences of impending disasters. The development of these signals is often beyond the capacities of individual organizations, but organizational leaders must avail themselves of relevant systematic information that can be secured from reliable external sources. This means that nonprofits need to have their antennae out and tuned to the appropriate channels. Some generic sources of current information on nonprofits, such as the *Chronicle of Philanthropy* or electronic newsletters issued by *Candid, Independent Sector* or the *National Council of Nonprofits*, may contain helpful warnings on broad issues such as economic recessions or national political or social crises, but hazards are often specific to nonprofits' particular circumstances. Just as for natural disasters where risks vary by location (for example, hurricanes in the South, fires in California, tornadoes in the Midwest), nonprofit risk profiles also vary with region or urban/ suburban rural location. Moreover, nonprofit vulnerabilities vary by the fields of service within which they operate. Thus, arts and cultural organizations are especially vulnerable to developments such as a pandemic or severe economic recession which restrict box-office sales, public health and social service organizations must be prepared for the inordinate demands of social disruption from a drug-related crisis or crime wave, and human service and educational institutions may be at risk in political crises that lead to constrictions of governmental funding. For each of their particular circumstances, nonprofits need to be alert to the probabilities and consequences of potential catastrophic developments such as those discussed in Chapter 2.

The president of the United States famously receives a daily briefing, first thing in the morning, on brewing issues and trouble spots. The resources to put such a report together on a day-to-day basis are considerable, involving information-gathering and monitoring across the federal government (and the world). A briefing on such a scale is generally beyond the reach of nonprofit executives, but something similar, scaled down to the needs of an individual organization and its information-gathering capacities, makes sense for non-profit leaders who need to know what is going on in the world beyond their doors and walls and internal systems of communication. They need a system of good road signs. Belonging to networks, as considered in Chapter 10, can provide some of the infrastructure to synthesize the information they need for weekly or monthly if not daily briefings. Suggested content for such a briefing is described below, based on the discussion in Chapter 2 and the threats that various kinds of crises pose for the prerequisites of organizational resilience, such as income, assets, human resources and network relationships.

The concept of a *dashboard* for internal management has a substantial history, mainly in the business sector. Dashboards allow leaders to monitor the organization's operations on a day-to-day basis, with gauges to signal where operations or resources may need shoring up and where they are adequate. Scales on these gauges or flashing indicators can signal danger levels that require particular or immediate attention. But what should these gauges be measuring in order to ensure resilience?

For one thing, dashboards can alert managers to the organizational implications of the general road signs they are reading about changes in their social, economic, political and policy environments. For example, if general sources of information suggest that poverty is worsening, they can monitor changes in demand for their social services, or if the economy is said to be slowing they can track changes in giving levels to their organizations. In these ways, managers can both stay abreast of broad environmental trends and begin to discern the implications of those trends for their particular circumstances. Below, we offer the construct of a monthly executive briefing (MEB), supplementary to a dashboard, to keep leaders abreast of environmental changes and their organizational implications.

More fundamentally, dashboards can help leaders track the various dimensions of resilience discussed throughout this book – assets and liabilities, cost structure, income portfolios, technological capacities, human resources, entrepreneurial skills and network relationships. These dimensions can be thought of in terms of "margins of organizational slack" or reserve capacities that should be maintained in normal times and drawn upon in times of crisis. It remains to put information on these elements together into dashboards that provide an effective overview of an organization's capacity to be resilient. Much of this chapter is devoted to building that construct. It is unlikely that a suitable, single measure can be synthesized in the form of an overall resilience index, but a well-constructed dashboard can assist experienced nonprofit leaders in grasping the general resilience of their organizations at any given time or in any circumstance. In its multidimensionality, the dashboard concept is consistent with the "balanced scorecard" approach commonly used in strategic planning for businesses and sometimes nonprofits as well (Balanced Scorecard Institute, 2021a). The basic idea is to broaden the notion of organizational performance to include nonfinancial as well as financial measures. Indeed, the dashboard construct is often used within the framework of the balanced scorecard approach (Balanced Scorecard Institute, 2021b).

In his path-breaking work on managing the performance of social enterprises, Paton (2003) offers a dashboard template for social enterprises. His dashboard has five boxes (picture dials on a dashboard) which monitor various aspects of organizational performance, two of which display essential information for resilience management. The "Risk" box monitors ways in which the enterprise might be put in jeopardy; for example, via a liquidity crisis, nonconformance to a legal or procedural requirement, or a breakdown in key relationships. The "Assets & Capabilities" box monitors the organization's capacity to deliver future performance, including physical and financial assets, external reputation and relationships, and expertise and process knowledge. It is easy to extrapolate these risk and capacity indicators to the parameters of resilience management discussed in various parts of this book. Risks could include the various economic, human resource, technological, leadership and relational breakdowns that might occur in a crisis, while assets and capabilities reflect the resources and slack that would be available to respond to crisis situations.

Below, we offer our own dashboard prototype to monitor parameters that reflect the adequacy of organizational slack and capacity along the various dimensions of risk and resilience discussed in chapters 4 through 10.

STRESS TESTS

Stress testing is an engineering approach that derives from procedures to determine the limits of machines or materials. Concrete or steel are stress-tested for their ultimate strength under load, and cars and airplanes are stress-tested to see how fast or how long they can operate under various environmental conditions before they fail. In commerce, stress testing through simulation has been applied to organizations to assess the limits of their economic viability under alternative market assumptions. Famously, large banks in the United States were stress-tested after the financial crisis of 2008–2009 in order to ensure their viability going forward. More generally, stress testing is integral to the regulatory framework of financial institutions in the United States (Kenton, 2021). In particular, the Federal Reserve requires banks with $100 billion or more in assets to perform stress tests, which usually involve determining whether the banks have adequate reserves to cover demands for funds in various kinds of crisis situations.

Stress testing of organizations depends on the art of "scenario planning," where the focus is on the question "What if?" This requires identifying potential catastrophes that could conceivably occur, determining through simulation and analysis what the impacts would be on the organization, specifying how the organization could respond, and calculating if such response would suffice to ensure survival and viability.

As noted in Chapter 2, it is virtually impossible to anticipate everything that could possibly go wrong. Indeed, an important aspect of nonprofit resilience management is the ability to cope with the unexpected. However, an organization can certainly examine its critical infrastructure and ask itself what would happen and what could be done if, for any reason, components of that infrastructure should fail. Along those lines, we examine below how to apply stress tests to failures of the balance sheet, the cost structure, the income portfolio, the technology in use, human resource practices, entrepreneurial problem-solving capacity and the network of external collaborative relationships. This is a much more comprehensive and multifaceted approach to stress testing than simply running alternative financial scenarios. However, as the chapters in this book have argued, resilience is a much more robust concept then simply financial capacity; thus, comprehensive multidimensional stress testing is requisite to resilience, fully conceived.

TEMPLATE FOR A MONTHLY EXECUTIVE BRIEFING

As the life of a typical nonprofit executive is increasingly hectic, a daily briefing on threats and impending crises is too much to ask of the executive's time or of her organization's capacity. At the same time, the more leisurely pace of an annual or five-year environmental scan associated with conventional strategic planning would not reflect the speed and urgency with which a crisis can develop. Recent examples such as the financial meltdown of 2008–2009 or the COVID-19 pandemic are instructive. Once identified in their nascent stages they grew rapidly in urgency. At first, the trends had to be monitored periodically, until the crisis erupted, at which point daily monitoring was needed. The point of the executive briefing would be to alert nonprofit leaders to the pending crisis, before the organization is required to switch into crisis mode with all hands on deck, just as road signs are intended as warnings to prevent an accident from happening. As a nominal recommendation, an MEB would seem both feasible and desirable, although every organization should adjust this guideline to its own circumstances, and briefings can become more frequent in a time of crisis.

What information would the MEB contain, assuming that it should be brief and specific to accommodate demands on executive time? As suggested in Table 11.1, for illustration, the MEB should identify impending threats in different broad categories, describe the organizational vulnerabilities associated with those threats, provide a preliminary assessment of the likelihood that the threat will manifest itself, and recommend possible (preventive) actions that could be considered at the present time. Succeeding MEBs would update these assessments, drop those that have dissipated and add new ones as needed, all within the time and resources that the organization is reasonably able to devote to it. Large organizations might develop the MEB in some depth; smaller ones could be more succinct. And all organizations should customize them to their particular circumstances.

A TEMPLATE FOR DASHBOARDS

A resiliency dashboard should help the nonprofit executive monitor the organization's various margins of resilience and flash warnings when margins are too low. Following the logic of chapters 4 through 10, a dashboard might contain the following indicators, as sketched in Table 11.2. The first column specifies the various dimensions in which nonprofit organizations can manage their levels of slack and contingency resources. The second column suggests the kinds of things that can measured in order to assess the levels of slack and hence the opportunity to respond robustly to crises. The third column suggests the criteria for flashing warning lights when those levels of reserve are dangerously low. Some of the rows are better developed than others, because research on the financial aspects of nonprofit performance is currently more advanced than it is for nonfinancial performance measurement. For example, indicators such as the number of months of operating reserve funds, or the Herfindahl–Hirschman Index (HHI) of concentration (diversification) of income sources, are already well established in practice and research. More broadly, analysts cite an array of ratios comparing assets, liabilities, income and expenses, and so on, that can be used to assess financial risk in a nonprofit organization (Greenlee and Tuckman, 2007, p.324).Organizations can develop many of the other measures for themselves, given sufficient attention and introspection. Over time, improvements can be made in such dashboards including streamlining and simplification, as experience is gained in their use. For example, with sufficient analysis, a system of red, orange and green lights might be engineered to alert the busy executive to areas that need immediate attention (red), require monitoring (orange) or are OK for now (green). Those areas flashing red can be examined in further detail to determine what exactly the trouble might be. For example, if *Human Resources* is flashing red, the problem could be low morale or low levels of volunteer involvement that threaten capacity for resilience in a crisis. Used in this way, the dashboard construct offers substantial potential for putting nonprofit leaders in the driver's seat when it comes to crisis readiness, preparation and ultimately navigation.

Table 11.2   Dashboard gauges and warning lights

Resilience margin	Indicators	Danger zone	Sources of data
Balance sheet	Reserve funds Net assets Liquidity Lines of credit	Below X months of operating expense Negative net assets Low proportion of unrestricted net assets; low ratio of cash to investments Low credit limit relative to assets	Numbers gleaned from current financial reports
Income	Diversification Ratio of fixed to variable revenue Unexploited benefits Changes in contractual reimbursements relative to costs of provision	HHI near 1; high proportion of income from the largest source Low fixed to variable income ratio Low income to benefit ratio Falling reimbursement to cost ratio for services rendered	Calculated from income statements Benefit theory assessment Income and expense statements
Costs	Ratio of fixed to variable cost Prospective economies of scope and scale Changes in costs of essential inputs	High fixed to variable cost ratio Lack of cost-saving expansion opportunities Prices compared to general rate of inflation	Estimated from budget data and cost analysis Government data and expense statements
Human resources	Ratio of salaried to contract workers Ratio of paid staff to volunteers Staff and volunteer morale Staff workload	High ratio of salaried to contract workers High ratio of paid to volunteer staff Indicators of low morale and high turnover Increases over normal workload	Calculated from human resources administrative reports, workload analysis, and surveys of worker satisfaction and morale
Technology	Proportion of output that could be provided by an alternative technology Number of prospective innovations in the queue Mechanisms for double-loop learning (for further details on double-loop learning, please see Chapter 3)	Low ratio of alternative to current output Few innovations actively planned Lack of mechanisms to integrate experience into change	Special reviews by management staff or consultants
Networks	Number of network affiliations Redundancy of similar ties Proportion of network affiliations that are reciprocal Ratio of strong to weak ties	Few memberships and agreements with external organizations Lack of duplication in key areas such as fund development, advocacy and mutual learning Low ratio of reciprocal to total affiliations Imbalance of strong vs weak ties	Special management assessments by staff or consultants
Entrepreneurial capacity	Autonomy level of division managers Mechanisms for staff and volunteers to contribute ideas and solve problems Underutilized assets Internal sources of venture capital	Highly centralized decision making Low staff participation in brainstorming and idea-generation Little slack in asset and facility uses Low ratio of uncommitted to committed capital	Special management reviews and staff surveys

A TEMPLATE FOR STRESS TESTS

As with dashboards for monitoring current conditions, stress tests can evaluate possible future circumstances by simulating the impacts of crises on the various margins of organizational slack. In particular, stress tests address the "what if" questions with respect to each of these margins, as illustrated in Table 11.3.

Table 11.3   Stress tests

Resilience margin	What if a crisis causes …?	Likely short-term response	Impacts/likely scenario	Preventive actions
Balance sheet	Market value of financial investments to tank	Reduce costs and services; tap reserves	Possible downward spiral; continued contraction of operations	Diversify assets; build reserves
Income	Main source of operating income to be cut off	Reduce costs and services; intensify fundraising	Existential threat; reduced mission effectiveness	Develop alternative sources; review cost and revenue structure
Costs	Building maintenance costs to spike	Borrow funds or use reserves; defer maintenance	Deterioration of service; safety hazards; regulatory and liability problems	Consider moving to rental space; capital campaign to upgrade facility
Human resources	Budget shortfalls from revenue loss	Layoffs, furloughs, pay cuts	Loss of staff morale and capacity, deterioration of services	Realign workforce combination of salaried, contractual and volunteer workers; seek new sources of income
Technology	Internet to fail	Curtailment of services; scramble to provide alternative services	Losses of income; client disaffection	Invest in alternative technologies; innovate to accomplish mission in different ways; build redundancy
Networks	Federation support to be curtailed	Budget reductions and reallocations	Deterioration of services	Join more networks; develop alternative sources of income
Entrepreneurial capacity	Innovation fund to shrink	Reassignment or reduction of staff; elimination of experimental programs	Loss of morale, dynamism and effectiveness over time	Join collaborative networks; revisit annual budget allocation process
Multiple impacts	Margins of slack impacted along multiple dimensions; e.g., income, assets and human resources	Multi-pronged short-term amelioration tactics	Multiple dimensions of loss and deterioration	Comprehensive rebuilding plan

In this table, stress tests are envisioned along each margin as well as in combinations along multiple dimensions such as assets, income and human resources. These tests can be designed on the basis of multiple anticipated scenarios associated with hazards that the organization realistically faces. For example, a community care organization in the Southwestern United States might anticipate the possibility of an extreme heat wave that could severely impact its energy costs, threaten its ability to serve clients (and hence its revenue streams) and damage its assets through fire and heat damage. It would therefore want to determine how resilient it would be in such circumstances by simulating its short-term response (column 3) and longer-term developments that would follow (column 4) in order to formulate a preventive or ameliorative strategy (column 5). Any single organization should specify multiple stress tests according to the particular set of hazards it anticipates confronting. Depending on organizational capacity, such tests might be performed on a rolling annual or biannual basis, with different margins of resilience examined each year. Smaller organizations might engage board members or pro bono consultants to keep costs down and exploit their independent perspectives (and indeed their responsibilities as trustees). The important thing is for leaders to maintain a consciousness about resilience-related vulnerabilities even if their analyses are rudimentary.

This approach does not fully protect against crises in which the organization is blind-sided (black swan events), but if multiple hazards are analyzed in this way, the approach has the virtue of covering most of the sources (margins of slack) that will need to be mobilized in any catastrophic situation. On the brighter side, working through stress tests can be a collaborative, team-building effort of staff and board members, itself strengthening the organization's morale and capacity for everyday performance as well as long-term resilience.

SUMMARY

In various chapters, including 3, 7 and 9, we have alluded to the importance of nonprofit organizations becoming "learning organizations" with cultures, policies and procedures that permit them to improve over time by carefully assessing current performance and past failures, and applying these lessons to future policies and procedures. In this chapter we have described various ways in which nonprofits can conduct their assessments of current performance and vulnerabilities, impending risks and capacity for resilience. In this way, nonprofits can develop themselves as learning organizations by following the data generated by dashboards and stress tests, in order to make current adjustments in their operations and build their informational infrastructure for the future.

We have observed here that only certain areas of information generation related to resilience are currently well understood and accessible in most nonprofit organizations. Essentially, competently run nonprofits will already have reasonably good access to financial information that can help provide guidance on asset, liability and income-related strategies. However, other margins of slack are typically not well documented and will require the development of new data streams and reporting formats. As suggested in Table 11.2, this holds true in some substantial measure for cost, human resources, technology, networks and entrepreneurial capacity information. Suitable reporting on cost and human resources resilience should be relatively easy to assemble from existing, routine management data collected outside the financial area. However, necessary information on network, technology and entrepreneurial dimensions of resilience require new data-collection and reporting structures. Most importantly, these efforts must be customized to the particular needs, vulnerabilities and capacities of individual organizations. Smaller organizations may wish to develop very modest informational systems consistent with their resource constraints, and they may decide to draw on external consultants or the expertise of their board members to help. Larger organizations may be able to develop more elaborate systems, using internal staff and board capacity, and technical consultants. The main point, however, is that leadership must begin to focus on resilience by creating informational structures that direct their attention to organizational risks and capacities to address those risks. More than this, the development and use of such informational resources can be viewed as a strategic opportunity to stimulate discourse among stakeholders in the organization so that all are on board with decisions to build resilience and navigate crises when they do occur (Paton, 2003).

REFERENCES

Balanced Scorecard Institute (2021a). "Balanced Scorecard Basics." https://balancedscorecard.org/bsc-basics-overview/.

Balanced Scorecard Institute (2021b). "Webinar: Using Dashboards to Bring Strategy to Life." https://balancedscorecard.org/bsc-basics/articles-videos/webinar-using-dashboards-to-bring-strategy-to-life.

Commission to Examine Nonprofit Human Services Organization Closures (2016). *New York Nonprofits in the Aftermath of FEGS: A Call to Action.* https://humanservicescouncil.org/wp-content/uploads/Initiatives/HSCCommission/HSCCommissionReport.pdf?q=commission/hsccommissionreport.pdf.

Flynn, Daniel, and Yunhe (Evelyn) Tian (2014). "The Death of Hull House." *Nonprofit Quarterly.* Winter.

Greenlee, Janet S., and Howard Tuckman (2007). "Financial Health," chapter 14 in Dennis R. Young (ed.), *Financing Nonprofits.* Lanham, MD: AltaMira Press, pp.315–335.

Kenton, Will (2021). "Stress Testing." Investopedia. www.investopedia.com/terms/s/stresstesting.asp.

Paton, Rob (2003). *Managing and Measuring Social Enterprises.* London: SAGE.

Cartoon 12   This one is just right!

12. A new paradigm for nonprofit management: the Goldilocks approach

We have argued from the start that in today's environment of uncertainty and recurring, yet often unanticipated crises, a new approach to managing nonprofit organizations is needed. In particular, in order for their organizations to remain viable and effective, nonprofit managers and leaders need to focus on the resilience of their organizations over time rather than their short-time performance or "efficiency." There are several reasons for this. First, "efficiency" is often very narrowly interpreted to mean "austerity," implying that nonprofits should use a minimum of resources to carry out their missions. Such austerity is somehow considered virtuous because it is argued that that is what "charitable" institutions are supposed to do. This, on its face, is a bad idea because it deprives society of the benefits nonprofits could produce if they were fully resourced, and because it makes them fragile and highly vulnerable to crises.

A slightly more generous interpretation of the efficiency notion is that nonprofits should achieve maximum results on a day-to-day basis with whatever resources they can command. In this view, reserves, overhead and administrative costs are seen as wasteful above a certain minimum, and all focus is put on current output or immediate outcomes. While such "streamlined" operation may seem virtuous, it neglects the need for nonprofits to cope with emergencies and catastrophic events, not to mention achieving longer-term impacts. In particular, when a nonprofit fails in a crisis, society may incur a substantial opportunity cost in the form of future services and benefits not provided, if responsibility for those services and benefits is not picked up by another provider.

A classical interpretation of efficiency, used by economists, is the optimal allocation of resources among alternative uses. This would take into account the risks that nonprofit organizations continually face *and* their performance over the long run. In an ideal world of perfect information and managerial wisdom and foresight, this view of efficiency would be appropriate for guiding nonprofit decision making. It would lead to an allocation of resources that would maximize the expected net benefits that nonprofits are able to provide for society through time. Unfortunately, we do not live in such a world, because information is never perfect, and judgment and analysis are always potentially flawed. The best we can do is to aim for long-run efficiency, properly interpreted, factoring in risks, while making provisions for being surprised and having the capacity to adapt to whatever new circumstances present themselves.

This is where managing for resilience differs from managing for efficiency. As we have considered throughout this book, nonprofit organizations must have both margins for error and the reserve capacities to utilize those margins so that they are able to adapt and remain viable and effective over time. This idea plays itself out throughout the chapters of this book, because there are multiple dimensions along which nonprofits can and should hedge their bets – in their capital structure, in their cost structure, in their income portfolios, in their technologies, in their workforces and in their network relationships with other organizations. And to do this, they need certain explicit capacities for resilience management, including an entrepreneurial problem-solving culture and an information system that warns them about approaching problems and continually gauges their capabilities for dealing with them.

The good news here is that nonprofits that manage for resilience in preparation for future crises will also be better positioned to perform well in ordinary times. In particular, the "slack" that is built for crisis situations, in forms such as robust staff capacity, financial reserves, alternative technologies, multiple income streams, contingent cost structures and robust networks, would not sit idle but may be engaged to help nonprofits innovate, experiment and plan for the future – in short, to develop as more effective organizations in the present.

Finally, we need to recognize nonprofits for the special roles they play in society – not just as providers of critical services or promoters of social causes and goals, but rather as institutions that we wish to be available to us when needed, whenever that may be. Unlike for-profit businesses which come and go with limited regret – yes, even our favorite restaurants, movie theaters and grocery stores are transient – nonprofits like museums, symphonies, hospitals, universities, YMCAs or Jewish Community Centers, community health clinics, and community centers and libraries call for a certain permanence and dependability that requires resilience, however their efficiency may be conceived or measured.

PREPARATION VERSUS NAVIGATION

We have noted throughout this volume that there are two basic parts to resilience management: preparing for crises and navigating through them. It is with this realization that the concept of reserves, redundancy and organizational slack comes into play. Broadly conceived, preparation for crisis requires building appropriate levels of slack while navigation requires the utilization of available slack to manage through a crisis and come out whole or even stronger at the end of it.

Table 12.1   *Strategies to prepare for and navigate crises*

Strategy area	Preparing for crises	Navigating crises
Balance sheet	Build reserve funds and lines of credit; increase liquidity	Apply liquid assets and credit to cover deficits and emergency expenses
Cost structure	Increase the ratio of variable to fixed costs; identify possible economies of scale and scope	Adjust variable costs in tandem with changes (losses) in output and revenue; consider collaborations and mergers
Income portfolio	Apply benefits theory to diversify and broaden income base	Compensate for losses of some income streams by relying on alternatives
Human resources	Develop and engage flexible forms of labor employment to control size of workforce (e.g., volunteers, contract work)	Utilize workforce flexibility to adjust size of workforce to meet crisis conditions
Technology	Develop backup technologies for mission delivery; invest in innovation	Ramp up alternative technologies if primary mode is restricted by crisis
Networks	Cultivate multiple network relationships, especially reciprocal links; build advocacy coalitions	Seek assistance from reciprocal networks, including federations, philanthropy and government
Entrepreneurship	Build internal culture of entrepreneurship and innovation	Engage in creative problem-solving to address issues posed by crisis

Table 12.1 operationalizes this principle by applying some of the lessons of earlier chapters to the two stages of nonprofit resilience management. The table briefly summarizes a few of the strategies available in each case. The reader is invited to elaborate on it by developing more detail on the actions described in the cells of the second and third columns.

HOW MUCH SLACK? THE GOLDILOCKS PRINCIPLE

Can we go further than to simply prescribe in qualitative terms the preparations listed in column 2 of Table 12.1? In particular, how much slack, reserve or redundancy should be sought along each of these lines of strategic preparation for a crisis? How big a reserve fund? How large a line of credit? How much more emphasis on variable versus fixed costs? How much more diversification into alternative income streams? What proportions of flexible workforce components such as contract workers and volunteers? How many backup technologies? How many network engagements and how intense should they be? How much internal investment in innovation and entrepreneurship capacity? These are all complex questions that require individual attention, as discussion in earlier chapters indicates. However, we can offer some unifying guidelines for all of these questions.

First, they all involve decisions about levels of organizational slack. Establishing commitment to prudent levels of slack is the first important step towards effective resilience management. Second, it must be recognized that extreme answers to the question of how much slack should exist are imprudent.

Zero slack risks fragility and disaster in a crisis, a basic premise of this book. But too much slack is wasteful and can involve serious opportunity costs by causing organizations to fall short of their potential ability to address their social missions. This is where the Goldilocks principle applies. Simply put:

> For management decisions involving the allocation of resources, levels of slack should be large enough to assure resilience but not so large as to be wasteful.

A snappier way of saying this is the motto "Slack, not sloth!" In practice, what does this look like?

SLACK VERSUS SLOTH: WHAT LEVEL OF SLACK IS JUST RIGHT?

There are no absolute, quantitative answers to this question, for several reasons. First, there are serious technical problems associated with the measurement of some of the dimensions of slack or redundancy as described in the table and in earlier chapters. While some indicators may be clear or straightforward – for example, months of cash in a reserve fund, or ratios of variable costs to fixed costs – others, such as entrepreneurial capacity or technological redundancy, are not so obvious. Second, there is no objective standard for specifying appropriate levels of slack. While rules of thumb such as "six months of operating expenses" or "less than half of income should come from any one source" can be suggested as good practice based on individual experiences, such rules are not scientifically established nor even formulated for most areas of nonprofit strategic decision making. It is not even clear how such rules would be formulated, except by consensus among experienced nonprofit managers in different service fields and circumstances. Even then, the rules would be subjective, albeit possibly comforting to perplexed nonprofit leaders and managers.

But in fact, recognizing the subjectivity of these decisions is a step forward, again for two reasons. First, it puts the focus where it belongs – on the managers and leaders responsible for these strategic decisions. Second, it suggests a way for making these judgments based on leaders' own assessments and attitudes towards the risk their organizations face. How can we operationalize these ideas? How can leaders determine the Goldilocks levels of strategic slack that is right for their organizations?

Consider the following generic choice for the level of strategic slack (S) in any given row of Table 12.1. The manager must choose between employing that level of slack to keep her organization safe or engaging in a lottery with no such level of strategic slack (see Figure 12.1). In this "lottery" there is a small probability (p) that a serious crisis will occur, creating a catastrophic loss (L). On the other hand, there is a high probability (*1 minus p*) that no such catastrophic event will occur, in which case the organization would operate effectively, devoting all its resources to directly achieving its mission. The values for p and L are subjective in the sense that the manager will have to employ the best thinking of staff and others to make a sensible estimate. More to the point, however, is that the decision itself is subjective. Engaging their own best judgments and individual attitudes towards risk, managers need to ask themselves: *What value of S would make me (or our organization) indifferent to the choice between slack and no slack?* For example, how large a reserve fund would we need in order to feel that we are as well off as we would be if we were unprotected with reserves and just took our chances? Or, how much emphasis should we put on a second revenue source in order to feel as well off as when we rely solely on our principal source of income? Certainly, the value of S should not be so large as to seriously compromise normal performance, nor should it be so small that its presence fails to achieve a state of operation that is more comfortable than going without a reserve or a second source of income. Call the answers to this introspective question Sg – the Goldilocks levels of strategic slack.

CHANGES IN PRACTICE

The resilience approach will require important changes in conventional practice with respect to the management, governance, financing, accounting and regulation of nonprofit organizations and the way we educate nonprofit managers and leaders. Such changes must derive from a new understanding of nonprofit organizations and the circumstances of their operations. Nonprofits must be understood as *venerable* institutions whose preservation and integrity

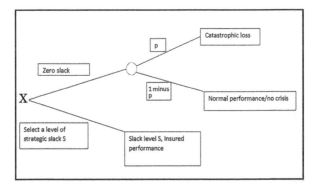

Figure 12.1   Estimating the Goldilocks levels of slack

are essential to proper functioning of our society. We must ensure that they be there when needed to serve our health, welfare, aesthetic and environmental needs, and our democratic and charitable impulses. Yet they are also *vulnerable* institutions which operate increasingly at risk of catastrophes and crises, mostly not of their own making. With this understanding, the new focus must be on preserving organizational integrity and fortifying nonprofits to perform well over the long haul and in the face of various known and unknown risks and possible catastrophic circumstances. Short-run views of "maximum bang for the buck," or austere practices to ensure charitable virtue, must necessarily yield to a pragmatic notion of viability that allows nonprofits to engage a prudent level of slack that can be drawn upon when dire circumstances prevail. As the chapters of this book have described, this point of view translates into some very specific guidelines for future practice, including:

* Adequate financial reserves and access to credit;
* Nimble cost structures;
* Diversified income portfolios and crisis-resistant forms of income;
* Redundant technologies;
* Rich collaborative networks;
* Flexibly structured and motivated workforces;
* An entrepreneurial problem-solving culture;
* A learning environment driven by systematic attention to data.

The implementation of these practices will require changes in nonprofit institutions and behaviors across the board. In particular:

* Educators must revamp their curricula and approaches to teaching nonprofit management and leadership.
* Regulators and rating agencies must reconstruct their standards to acknowledge the importance of prudent slack management, not only in financial terms but across the multiple dimensions of nonprofit management.
* Trustees must guarantee that their organizations have adequate slack resources to ensure their long-term integrity and viability.
* Foundations, government and other funders must reward their nonprofit grantees and contractors for resilience planning and practices, rather than incentivize short-term effectiveness or lowest-cost operation.
* Managers must manage for resilience along all dimensions where their organizations can be fragile and vulnerable, and they must take the long view of their performance and the environments in which they operate.

TRUSTEES, FUNDERS AND REGULATORS

While this book has been written with nonprofit executives specifically in mind, it is abundantly clear that these leaders cannot achieve resilience of their organizations by themselves. In particular, governing boards, funders, and regulators and rating agencies must all step up their game. Governing boards are especially critical. The mindset of trustees must be to preserve and enhance the capacity of their organizations to achieve their missions over the long term. This means working with their executives more at the strategic than operational level, helping them to put the resources and systems in place for building resilience, and overcoming temptations to squeeze out short-term cost savings at the expense of long-term viability. It also means taking a broader view of their responsibilities to preserve the integrity of their organizations, not only ensuring honesty, good behavior and transparency on a quarterly or semi-annually basis but taking responsibility for performance into an indefinite future. This is entirely consistent with the legal and long-accepted principles of trusteeship, and not radical reform of governance practices so much as a re-examination in the context of resilience management.

Funders, including foundations, major donors and government agencies, should also refocus their efforts and practices, to help nonprofit leaders make their organizations more resilient. This includes re-examining policies concerning funding of administrative capacity, design of reimbursement to cover costs, avoiding unnecessary restrictions on gifts and grants, and encouraging diversified income portfolios. Funders can also help nonprofits build the infrastructure they need to alert them to risk and vulnerabilities and to better gauge their performance over the long term.

Regulators and rating agencies can be helpful as well. Arbitrary ratio standards that can misguide donors should be phased out in favor of more comprehensive assessments of resilience measures including balance sheet health, income diversification, nimbleness of cost structures, technological capacities, network strength, entrepreneurial leadership, workforce health and flexibility, and informational infrastructure to signal risk and vulnerability and operate as a learning organization over time. It will require creativity and hard work to move from the "quick and dirty" signals that rating agencies now provide to donors, to emulate the rich information that investors are entitled to in the business sector. This is another area where funders can help. Such an investment in the resilience of nonprofit organizations would be highly worthwhile.

Finally, educators have an important supportive role to play as well. Nonprofit management education curricula, in schools of public policy and administration, social work, business, management, philanthropy or other auspices, must be re-oriented and rebuilt in ways that help prepare the coming generations of nonprofit managers and leaders for the turbulence they are likely to face, the ways they can turn crisis into opportunity, and the prudent strategies of organizational slack available to achieve long-run organizational excellence and success in addressing their social missions.

Hopefully, the three bears (regulators, funders and educators) will be sympathetic and supportive of nonprofit leaders' efforts to build resilient organizations. Long live Goldilocks!

SUMMARY

Resilience requires a broader understanding of efficiency, taking account of the manifold and serious risks that nonprofit organizations face, and the imperative to serve and succeed over the long run. However, managing for resilience is not a trade-off between short-term success and long-run resilience. Management practices designed for resilience serve to improve functioning and effectiveness in ordinary times as well. Resilience management involves both navigating crises at hand and preparing for future possible catastrophes as well. Distinctly different actions and capacities are required in each of these cases. Moreover, resilience strategies are multidimensional, involving not only an organization's finances, but its human resources, network relationships, technologies, entrepreneurial capacity and informational systems as well.

A common dimension of resilience strategies is their focus on developing and utilizing prudent levels of slack along these latter dimensions. A prudent level of slack allows an organization to respond to crises in the short term and can be employed in ordinary times to build the organization's long-term effectiveness. Determining prudent levels of slack should follow the Goldilocks principle: not so much to render the organization wasteful or ineffectual but enough to ensure resilience in a crisis.

Funders, raters and regulators, and educators all have important roles in helping nonprofit leaders achieve resilience for their organizations. Educators in particular must take the lead in transforming nonprofit management from its current preoccupations with day-to-day administration and short-term efficiency and effectiveness, to a new paradigm of nonprofit resilience management.

Index

Printed and bound by CPI Group (UK) Ltd, Croydon, CR0 4YY

16/04/2025

14658492-0002